To
Jillian
Enjoy!!!
Al Anderson
2012

GROWING UP
WRITING DOWN

Stories of a Farm Kid

Albert William "Al" Anderson

Edited by Nancy Morrison & Linda Grosskopf

Nancy Morrison

Linda Grosskopf

ISBN 978-0-9790169-3-6

Edited by:
Nancy Morrison & Linda Grosskopf
PO Box 85
Billings, MT 59103
www.wordwrightwomen.com

For additional copies of this book, contact:
Al Anderson
468 South Moore Lane
Billings, MT 59101
406-245-8466

$15 plus $5 S/H

Acknowledgements

When the time comes to start dealing out thanks, I have plenty of folks to thank. A project like this necessarily involves a number of people, and I am grateful to have been surrounded by great people my whole life.

I have to first thank my Swedish father,
for pointing me in the direction that he did.
He provided the guidance and my first blank book.

That said, special thanks must go to my Irish-English mother,
whose loving support provided needed encouragement.

My brother Ed also helped me along the way
with good brotherly advice—whether I wanted it or not!

Once married, my wife Mona, the only woman I ever loved,
gave encouragement to finish up the stories
I still wanted to get down.

In 2006, my son, Al, Jr., conspired with his right-hand assistant,
Jonie Head, to enter my stories into her computer, both to save for
posterity and to print out a wire-bound copy for me.
That was a wonderful surprise and allowed me to give
a few copies to friends and family.

A word of thanks to my editor, Nancy Morrison,
who pretty much insisted that I do this project—
not to make any money, but to finish a life-long work.

I also want to thank
Linda Grosskopf, Editor, *Western Ag Reporter*, and
Shelli Randles, Publisher, *The Times-Clarion,*
for printing my stories in those newspapers.

And, last but not least, my appreciation and thanks
to my loyal readers throughout the years,
who have made my writing such a rewarding experience.

Dedication

This book is dedicated to my family, both current and future generations, because family is the link that binds us together and makes all the everyday happenings important. Looking back over my life, I can plainly see that my family has been the most important aspect of my life.

In dedicating these stories to them, I hope they get inspired to write down their stories. Together we can preserve our family history for the future.

Introduction

One day in the summer of 1939, my dad brought home from town a leather-bound book. He handed it to me and said, "Fill this journal with your life on a daily basis, and your grandkids will never forget who you were, where you came from, and just how you became an American on the way to growing up."

I opened up the leather-bound book and thumbed through it— all 600 pages—it was the best present in my life! I had already been writing down lots of things I had encountered. Living through the end of the Depression and the Second World War provided me with many hardships, as well as a whole passel of everyday events, that I scratched out on pieces of paper, catalogue pages, magazines, and scraps of Christmas paper.

I had filled up—totally crammed full, like our farm silos—three Quaker Oatmeal boxes with these bits and scraps of paper and figured someday to put them in some order so they would be readable and fun to read. Every story and article on those bits of paper were based on things that actually took place that I was witness to, or was involved in, from 1937 until the early 1950s.

Al Anderson. 2011

As with anything written, the words always make more sense and have a deeper and memorable meaning to the writer than to the reader, but all of these short stories are enjoyable and under-standable. They follow my life from the age of nine in 1937 until 1953, when I married the only lady I have ever loved, Mona Jean Summers, in Roundup, Montana, on January 24. Read these stories with an open mind, and you might find yourself relating to quite a few.

Contents

Editor's Notes

For ten years or so, a great number of Al's stories have been printed in *The Times-Clarion*, Harlowton, Montana, where they have enjoyed a wide appreciation among its readers. The one question most readers often asked, however, was whether there was a book to purchase. That question is now answered with this volume.

I got acquainted with Al through his son, who is my accountant. In the way that things often happen, we were just visiting about book projects, when he suddenly said that I should "do" his dad's stories. He showed me a wire-bound booklet of 60 some stories—and I was hooked. Al met with me, and we decided to go forward with putting his stories in book format.

The true charm of this collection of stories is found in the simple and colloquial manner in which Al has written them down. If you consider that Al was just a teenager when most of these stories were written, it will give you a big appreciation for his early talents. Certainly, these stories should give you a desire to pen your own recollections, as well.

It becomes apparent, when reading these stories, that it isn't the headline events that make up the biggest part of our lives; it is the everyday mundane matters that provide the structure and fabric of our lives. However, those everyday events that made up our childhood are now no longer everyday events. In fact, the world has changed so rapidly that those events "back in the day" often seem to be very far removed from today's lifestyle.

I have been extremely lucky to be able to work with my sister— Linda Grosskopf, Editor, *Western Ag Reporter*—on a number of her book projects, and together we team up to preserve Montana history. It has been our focus to work with folks who are in the process of writing their memoirs, and because of our interest in this field, we have had the opportunity to help people with their personal histories, as well as larger Montana history projects.

I hope that, as you savor these stories, you will use them as inspiration to write your own history down—it is so much fun to read and, more importantly, it is a roadmap for your family to follow into the back roads of your history.

Foreword

Iwas born August 28, 1928, in a little farm house just outside of Charles City, Iowa. From what I later gathered, it was not an earth- or world-shattering event. I was the third of five children born to Arthur Albert and Marcella Adeline Baird Anderson: Edward Arthur was born February 26, 1925; Evelyn Rachel, October 14, 1926; Albert William, August 28, 1928; Thomas David, October 15, 1930; and John James, December 31, 1935.

Al's parents. 1922.
Adeline Baird Anderson.
B. January 25, 1903. D. February 17, 1962.
Arthur Albert Anderson.
B. November 14, 1898. D. June 11, 1964.

The doctor present at my birth, Dr. McQuillan, was about 45 years of age and used a buggy pulled by a sorrel horse for transportation. Years later, he recalled the event and said that I was determined to stay where I had begun and that he had to convince me to join the family through his use of birthing forceps.

As I grew up through the Thirties, I acquired a desire to read and I read everything I could—sometimes asking my mother about words I did not understand. She always encouraged me to write those words down and then use her old dictionary to find the meaning. Through this process, I acquired a good vocabulary and began to make notes of things that affected my thinking and direction in life. By the time I was 11, I had accumulated hundreds of notes about anything that seemed worth saving for future use. My older brother Ed helped me build and retain a separate vocabulary for words that held a double meaning, and he also supplied me with words not found in any dictionary—nor used in polite conversation!

My father, an engineer and super smart, encouraged my use of a journal for future reading. Growing up between 1928 and 1943 was a challenge: hard times and hard work. With my father gone most of the time on the train, I owe my mother—bless her goodness—for my attitude and feelings towards people and all of God's creatures.

I attended country schools until 1935 when I attended Lincoln School in Charles City, Iowa. I later attended Carville School in Carrville and Line School located north of Charles City. Since completing the eighth grade was the only required education at that time, I didn't continue on to higher school then. In November 1943, I travelled some and I ended up in Oregon, where I worked in the shipyards, both in Oregon and Washington. In August of 1944, when I was about 16, I moved to Roundup, Montana, and worked on the Milwaukee Railroad and at Kibble & Case.

After a stint of cowboying at the Top Hat Ranch in Two Dot, Montana, I decided to attend the Roundup High School in the fall of 1947. I graduated in the spring of 1949. I attended Eastern Montana College in Billings, Montana, from 1951 through 1953. In 1953, I married Mona Jean Summers, who was a coal miner's daughter from Roundup, Montana. We have lived in Billings, Montana, since then.

Part I

Adventures in Iowa

1928 – 1943

My Yesterdays

I like to think of the good old days
    Kerosene lamps and one-horse shays
        Ice-cold water from a hand dug well
            The Sunday peal of the big church bell
The cider press we used each fall
    The main street movies free to all
        Saturday shopping in the little town
            Free band concerts when the sun went down
The popcorn wagon by the downtown park
    Baseball games that lasted until dark
        The raft and swing at the swimming hole
            Heating stoves that burned wood and coal
The fresh clean air of a blackland farm
    The smell of hay and rows of corn
        The old steam engine with monstrous wheels
            Threshing crews and home-cooked meals
Everyone attending a one-room school
    The fear of teacher's twelve-inch rule
        Ignoring the girls that you like best
            Worrying for days about final tests
The one-act plays on a make-do stage
    Skipping school on snow-bound days
        The skating pond and big bonfire
            Homemade bread and apple cider
Box lunch socials at the country school
    Long sleigh rides behind shaggy mules
        The first long pants you finally wore
            And the thousand things that went before
This modern life moves awfully fast
    When you sit and think about the past
        This thing called progress is a real test
            And the good old days were still the best

1952

A Bully Named Milt

I spent three school terms, from the sixth through part of the eighth grade, in a one-room country school in Carrville, Iowa. In the fall of 1939, on the first day of school, I stood behind a huge, hairy farm kid, who was first in line to enter the school, and none of the other kids challenged him. His name was Milton, he was quite a bit taller than I was, and he had arms so long they almost drug on the grass. He wore a blue pair of overalls and riding boots, with a baseball cap on his head. And not one kid snickered or laughed as he walked up the stairs and into the school. I was about five feet tall, and he was at least six feet tall. We visited for a few minutes while standing in line, and he informed me that he was in charge of the playground; his job was to make sure all the rules of the school and Miss Crouse were followed to the letter or he would see to it that the infractions were dealt with. I listened to every word very carefully, and when the teacher opened the front door, I followed him into the room and sat right behind his chair.

I only spoke when I was spoken to...

I was only 11 years old, but I knew the rules from the fifth grade, and I didn't plan on having any lapse of memory. Milt, as he like to be called, had told me during lambing season that it was his job to pick up the ewes that wouldn't stand after lambing and to keep them on their feet. That was a tough job, and when he told me that he had lifted up an axle on an empty hay wagon to help his dad put a wheel on it, I didn't doubt him and knew that axle would have weighed at least 200 pounds. I just knew that we were going to be friends, at least on my part. I stayed away from him as much as I could and only talked to him when he spoke to me first. My impression of Milt was that he could eat dried field corn without cooking it and whip anything his size.

Right after school began, I became friends with a fourth-grader named Neil. He was quiet and scholarly and liked to read about the West. He told me he wanted to become a cowboy when he got out of school. We visited every chance we had, and I found out that he didn't like Milt "two cents' worth" and that he was quite afraid of him. He said that, the past year, Milt had picked on him all the time during every recess and that he began to stay in the schoolroom rather than go out to play. His said that Milt had pushed him off the merry-go-round several times and had grabbed a chain swing so he would fall out. Milt also made Neil pump water for his team of horses and feed them oats. One day, he brought a gallon of linseed oil and made Neil paint the wagon wheels for the whole week.

Neil said that he had thought about stealing some of his mom's alum and mixing it into the pail of soup that Milt brought every day. The only reason he didn't was Milt might croak sitting in school and scare the liver out of everyone. And, if he didn't croak, there would be heck to pay when he got back on his feet—Heaven help all of his schoolmates. Neil had put a few horse biscuits in Milt's jacket pocket the previous winter and never got caught—even Miss Crouse laughed about that. I heard her tell one of the parents that Milt was a big pussycat and strutted around like a big-wattled rooster with a huge brood of chicks under his wing. He was wary of Miss Crouse because the school board would not tolerate any sass to the teacher, and the penalty could be expulsion and sometimes a smack with the willow switch.

The day before school had let out in May of 1939, Milt had taken over the merry-go-round and spun it so fast that Neil slipped off and broke his left thumb. Neil never told anyone; he just wrapped it up in a handkerchief, and it hurt like the devil for about two weeks. The thumb had healed crooked and bent to the left, and he never forgave Milt for that. Neil also told me that Milt was spending his second year in the sixth grade and was dumber than a boar pig with no brains, failed all of the state exams, and ended up in the county courthouse jail after the nut had threatened to beat up the superintendent and then throw the teacher into the river. When they notified his dad about the problem, he wasn't too concerned, and all he said was, "Boys will be boys, and Milt is a good kid who just got mad." He said that he would have a talk with Milt when they got home. The sheriff let Milt out of jail, and his dad paid the $10 fine to the county.

Planning for revenge…

I learned quite a bit about Milt from Neil, and the more we talked, the more we felt we should even the score on the bully. We had to do something without getting caught and beat to a pulp—or something worse. I told my older brother Ed about the dirty tricks Milt had pulled on Neil and some of the other kids. Ed thought about all that for quite some time and then asked me if Milt ever drove a wagon to school. I told him that Milt one to school almost every day and let the horses graze in the playground. He also made Neil and I clean up the deposit they made every day and keep the playground clean.

Ed came up with a good plan to put Milt on the defensive and hopefully to get him to quit picking on the other kids. Ed told me to have Neil bring his big nut wrench to school the next day in his lunch sack and hide it out back by the woodshed. Then Neil and I were to take turns going to the outdoor toilet and, in the process, remove two of the wheel-retaining nuts from the wagon and throw them down the toilet. That way, as Milt started home with the wagon, those two wheels would fall off real quick, one at a time. We were to loosen the big retaining nuts on the other two wheels, too, and they would fall off later on. All farmers carried one spare nut wired to the bolster, and by removing two nuts, Milt would be kept busy trying to put the wheels back on. And when the fourth wheel tumbled, he would have to walk home to get some help with the wagon. I explained the plan to Neil, and he readily agreed with the plan, saying the big a** might rupture himself and it would serve him right.

The next morning, Neil had the wrench, and we hid it close to the wagon. During the day, we made several trips to the toilet and removed three of the nuts from the wagon. That was the longest day of the school year for Neil and me, and we could just hardly wait to follow Milt up the dirt road.

How sweet it is…

School let out at four o'clock, and Neil and I stood by the road, keeping an eye on the wagon. A few minutes later, Milt had the horses harnessed and hitched to the wagon, and he started up the road to his farm. After about 300 feet, the right front wheel fell off, and the axle drug a furrow in the road before Milt could stop the team. We could hear him swearing a blue streak, and he jumped down to see what went wrong. He stood there for a few moments, swearing and using adjectives Neil and I never used. We hid in the ditch and watched Milt retrieve the wheel and look for the nut, which he never found. Then he went over to the fence, found a loose post, and tore it away from the fence. Next, he gathered up several big rocks to pry against to lift the wagon up to slip on the wheel.

Neil whispered, "Holy cow, he sure ain't very smart. How in the dickens can he lift up the wagon, hold it up, and still slide the wheel on?" I told Neil that Milt would figure that out when he got the wheel axle up in the air. Milt pried the axle up and stood there looking at the wheel lying on the road, out of reach. After a few moments, he lowered the wagon back down and swore some more. Then he gathered up some big boulders, piling them by the axle so he could push them in. Then he pried the wagon up a second time, and when it was the right height, he tried to push the rocks under the axle with his foot. He couldn't reach the rocks, and even if he had, the wagon would not be high enough to put the wheel on. He stood there, holding the wagon in the air. He swore a few more adjectives and then lowered the wagon down again. He sat down on the side of the road, staring at the wagon.

Milt finally figured out that he would need longer fence posts, stacked high enough to slide the wheel on, that he could push under the axle with his foot. He spent quite a while finding posts that he could stack that wouldn't fall down. He placed them next to the axle and pried the wagon up again; holding the pry post down, he succeeded in shoving the posts under the axle. He got the wheel on the axle and unwired the spare nut from the bolster, spinning it on the threads. He was smiling as he climbed back onto the wagon seat, picked up the reins, and slapped the horses. The wagon lurched forward about 50 feet before dropping the right rear wheel into the dirt. Milt pulled the team to a halt and jumped down, swearing loudly and calling the wagon a "wore out piece of horse dung." Neil started to laugh, and I held my hand over his mouth.

Lucky for Milt, he had only travelled about 50 feet, and he had no trouble retrieving the rocks and posts he just used. After following the same routine he used putting on the first wheel, he had no retaining nut for the axle so he wound some wire around the end of the axle and climbed back onto the wagon, threatening the wagon with possible destruction when he got home. He slapped the horses once more, and the wagon started forward again. Neil remarked that Milt should have thrown the posts and rocks into the wagon, just in case. This time the wagon travelled about 500 feet before the left rear wheel fell off.

We had followed down the ditch, way behind Milt, and we heard him swearing again. He couldn't believe it was happening to him, of all people. He jumped down from the wagon and surveyed the wagon and the wheel for some time. Neil said he thought that Milt was figuring out that three wheels just didn't fall off a wagon without some help. Neil was right, and we watched Milt walk to the left front wheel and easily remove the nut with his fingers. He turned and stared back toward the school, not moving for about five minutes. He kicked the wheel real hard, swore, and then hopped around like a chicken with a sore toe. After a few minutes, he unhitched one of the horses and threw the harness into the wagon box. He unhitched the other horse and started towards home, leading the harnessed horse.

A real good lesson...

Neil and I were only about a half mile from the school, so we hurried back and took off for home. I told Ed what had happened, and he laughed and said, if Milt gave us kids any trouble, to let him know. The next morning at school, Milt never said a word. He just sat in the classroom reading and staring out the window, quiet as a mouse in a flour bin. Even the teacher kept watching Milt to see if he was ill. He looked at Neil and me every few minutes and then pulled out his pocket watch, wound it, and put it back.

Later on into the school year, he had asked some of the girls if they had seen anyone around his wagon, but got no response. From that day on, he didn't bully anyone and was somewhat civil to everybody. He passed that year on into the seventh grade.

In 1943, Milt joined the Navy and left for about three months. He came home at the end of August and came by our farm to visit. Dad and I talked with Milt for quite a while, and he had really grown up—for the better! He was really quiet and polite. He had supper with us and thanked us for our hospitality. As he got into his car to leave, he looked at me and grinned. He said to Dad, "That was a real good lesson that your son and his friend, Neil, taught me. I'll never forget that a bully never comes out on top."

He went Missing In Action (M.I.A.) in 1944, in the Pacific... another good farmer lost to the war.

1946

Flying Machines

When I was growing up on our farm in the 1930s, airplanes were a novelty and something rarely seen in the sky around our area. A few bi-planes were heard and seen from time to time, and they made us want to see them up close. One Saturday, my dad took my brother Ed and me to the nearest airport, and we were able to walk right up to the several planes on the field. Our neighbor, Art Miller, was also there with his wife Mola, and their son named Gustaf. Old Man Miller, as he was known, yearned to fly, and he told me that he thought he could build a flying machine without too much trouble. He purchased all the books available about World War I planes: the Fokker, the Spad, and the Sopwith. It seems that, after he had read them through a few times, he spent some time convincing Gus to help him draw up the plans and help with the airplane. One of his inducements was that Gus would be the first to fly.

The darned thing really looked like a plane...

One Saturday, Art sent Gus off to town to buy wire and nails, baby buggy wheels, and a few 1- by 10-inch pine planks. He also brought home a roll of wood slat snow fence. From a junkyard, they rounded up the best of the parts they thought they would need to build "her" sound. Art and Gus worked on that airplane off and on all of the summer of 1936, and the darned thing really looked like an airplane. It was built with wood and braced by wire. They used a low spring seat from an old John Deere and baby buggy wheels for the landing gear. They added a spring harrow tooth for the tail drag.

For power, Gus made a Model T crank with a welded extension shaft mounted on bearings so it would turn free. Welded to that was an old Do-All Rumely cooling fan about ten inches in diameter to create a good breeze when Gus turned the crank. Gus told me that he figured he could turn the shaft fast enough because, when he turned the crank, the wind really whistled past his head. He said that, once he got her airborne, he would just coast around through the sky.

Gus would be a fighter pilot...

With a touch of bravado coated with sincerity, Gus said he was really going to practice flying so he could be a fighter pilot when he graduated from the eighth grade. The airplane he helped build was no sleek fighter plane, but it was oddly good looking and weighed about a ton. The wings of the plane were 20 feet wide and rounded on the ends. They were made of two 1- by 10-inch pine boards planed smooth. The body was made of wiring slats 1/4 inch by 3-inch by 3-foot long and wired to the fuselage made of cardboard. The tail was made of 1-inch by 12-inch by 6-foot long pine board with half of a wooden barrel top mounted on top of the board on a pivot so it could turn. There was a rope tied to the fin so Gus could steer the plane once he got it into the air.

Gus practiced everyday turning the crank that would give "her" flight. Old Man Miller just sat in a chair bolted to a plank of wood and pretended that he was flying through the sky. He even talked of flying to New York City and maybe even to Paris. They finally got the thing built and decided that Gus would be the pilot to lift off from the barn roof because he was the smallest. When I had a chance, I told Gus that, without a motor of some kind, I didn't think it would fly. Gus showed me his arm muscle and remarked that he could fly anything. That Sunday, my brother Ed and I helped Gus and Old Man Miller pull the plane to the top of their barn with the help of a block and tackle. It was a hell of a chore because it weighed so much, but we finally got it up to the weather vane. We wired it to the weather vane with some barbed wire and blocked the buggy wheels with blocks of wood.

Gus is Heaven-bound…

Gus slowly climbed to the top of the barn and settled into the old John Deere seat. He started to turn the crank and had it going so fast we couldn't see the fan blades. When he was up to speed, he hollered, "Turn her loose! I'm Heaven-bound!" With Gus turning the fan as fast as he could, Ed pulled away the wooden blocks, and I cut the holding wires with a pair of pliers. The thing rolled down the sloped roof, and when it came to the edge, it fell straight down and broke all to pieces. All of the blades of the fan were bent backwards, and the shaft was buried about two feet into the ground. We hurried down to where Gus was laying on top of a manure pile, thinking he was probably dead. We stood around Gus for a minute, and then he groaned and tried to get up. We made him lay still until my mother came to help. Old Man Miller walked around and around the heap of wood shaking his head and muttering, "I just don't know why the darn thing didn't zoom up into the air. Maybe Gus just didn't turn the propeller fast enough."

Birds fly without a fan on their nose…

Gus recovered from his airplane ride, and after his leg healed up, he told me he thought the roof wasn't steep enough. "Next time," he said, "we'll take her up to the 100-foot bluff by the river and jump it off there. I'll get a bigger fan, and I know it will fly. Hell, man… birds fly without a fan on their nose."

Looking back now, I realize that the old saying that cousins shouldn't marry was a good rule. Art and Nola Miller were first cousins—and Gus was just plain nuts.

Box Socials

In the early 1940s, one of the fun times that farm families enjoyed was a fall get-together at the country school. All families eagerly looked forward to the social event of the year where everyone gathered to have a good supper and watch a one-act play starring all of the students. Every kid was part of the festivities, and there were lots of proud parents watching. The real reason behind the social event was to integrate all of the local farmers into a group atmosphere and meld them together into one big family of friends. Just being there promoted fellowship, and a lot of shy kids and parents were the better for attending. Since farm life was somewhat isolated due to the distances between farms, this was a chance to get to know everyone in the area. I was fortunate enough to be able to attend two of these delightful events before the lousy Japs started the war with the U.S.—1941 was the last year that box socials were held in our area at the Crossroads School.

Everything was messed up…

When that little Japanese runt wearing a stovepipe hat gave the okay to attack Pearl Harbor, he messed up everyone's lives. Life in rural areas changed dramatically, and the attitude of "tomorrow was always another day" was replaced by a "hurry up" attitude with everyone I knew. Everything and everybody rushed through each day like there was not gonna be a tomorrow. Even the threshing crews meant business and almost killed off the bundle haulers, trying to unload their loads and race back to the fields to load up and out-do the rest of the haulers. Accidents began to happen more frequently—some severe. Fingers were cut off, and one hauler lost a leg when he fell under a loaded hayrack. At the box social held that fall, there were quite a few injured farmers. One farmer with a broken arm had fallen off the hayrack, one had fallen when delivering wood to the steam engineer, and another had walked head-on into the 30-foot twisted drive belt, cutting the top part of one leg so bad that he had to wear a brace to walk. Gossip during the box social was mainly about the war and who to dislike the most: Adolph Hitler or Emperor Hirohito. I personally disliked both of those bellicose idiots and hoped they would face a terrible retribution.

The skit was a huge success...

The box social held in our school district was put together by our elderly teacher, Miss Crouse, with everyone volunteering to help. The grand event began at 6:00 p.m. and ended at 8:30 p.m. The last one-act play held in our school was a comedy consisting of a wheelbarrow and two bums, who argued who could push a wheelbarrow across the stage without dumping the rider onto the floor. I lost the bet to a kid named Loren Rodemaker when I tried to push him across the stage. I tipped it over, and Loren fell out and landed on the front row on a lady's ample lap. All she did was grab Loren, give him a big bear hug, and help him back onto the stage. The audience roared with laughter, and the skit was a huge success.

The next part of the social was the one thing everyone really waited for. Each lady present had put together a box lunch—most used shoe boxes. She would wrap the box in pretty paper, and tie it up with ribbons. Each tried to have the prettiest box, but everyone knew that all food would be delicious: beef and pork sandwiches, pickles, a slab of apple or peach pie, and even muffins with chocolate frosting as a special treat. The school furnished coffee, milk, Kool-aid, and ice cream. The boxes were placed on a long table and were auctioned off to the highest bidder. The identity of the boxes was on a list and kept secret by Miss Crouse. As each lunch was bid out, it was opened by the successful bidder, who discovered the name written on the inside of the lid. He would then gather up his lunch partner, and they would sit together at one of the tables set up just for the occasion. No students were allowed to bid on the boxes, which wasn't a problem since the kids didn't have any money, and besides, who wanted to eat with a girl that might have fleas, cowpox, or scabies?

Candy bars for bribes…

A few days before the social event, everyone who would attend started to bribe the school kids with candy bars and money to reveal the names of the colored boxes to be bid on. Everyone tried to outbid every other bidder except those bidding on their own wife's box. There was one elderly farmer who knew the color of his wife's box, and he disrupted the bidding, as everyone thought he was bidding on someone's box that was extra special. That box was won by the farmer, and he then announced that it was his wife's lunch, and since she fixed everything he liked, he just couldn't let anyone else have his dinner! Everyone laughed and clapped, and that ended that bid.

Al and his sister Evelyn at the Nashua Fair, Iowa. August 1938.

Several of the unmarried farmers approached me and did their utmost to pry from me the color of my sister's box—money and candy being the barter items. Most of the un-hitched men liked Evelyn, but she had a steady boyfriend already. I had bragged that I knew her box lunch, but I really didn't have a clue.

Most of the lunches were sold for $3 to $4, but my sister's and one of the neighbor's older daughter's were both bid up to $10. Those two were the most expensive lunches. The teacher's lunch went for $5 to an older bachelor, who made the mistake of scratching his head during the bidding!

Pranks for one and all...

Everyone had a good time, and lots of laughter resulted from a bunch of pranks. Some unknown kid nailed the toilet door shut, and it took two hefty men to get it open. Someone threw all the Sears and Roebuck and Montgomery Ward catalogs down the toilet. Lucky for everyone, the teacher had some tissue that was available. One of the younger ladies complained that someone had covered the toilet with cracked corn, and an older lady said that someone threw dirt clods while she was inside. She said it scared her half to death because she thought the toilet was caving in. She stood up after the lunch and said, "You youngsters should be ashamed of all that ruckus," but no one confessed, and no one felt too ashamed!

The social began to disperse at 8:30 p.m. when the adults rounded up their broods and began to drive off. That usually took quite a while because they were all engaged in games like Hide and Seek, Who's Got the Ball, and Post Office for the upper kids—that was the favorite of all the girls. Some of the adults left early, and then there were always pranks played by the older kids. Soaped car windows, grease on the car door handles, and blocks of wood under the wheels of the cars were favorites. No one ever got mad, and parting was a friendly occasion. The event was discussed by the kids at the next school day. One of the topics most discussed was which was the best tasting: dried corn silk made with newspaper or not-quite-dried silk made with notebook paper. It wasn't habit forming, and it sure put out a real sore throat.

The subject of "corn squeezin's" brought by the younger farmers was bantered about, and it was decided that it didn't hurt to have a sip or two; but the old geezer who fell asleep and snored during the bidding was a fright. The teacher's big shepherd watchdog was chained to the front steps. He got to partake of all the leftovers, and there were always a lot of those. A hobo had sneaked up the porch and tried to steal the dog's lunch. He probably would have been successful, except he tried it while the dog was eating. The dog attacked him, and I got out of the door just in time to see the bum running down the Milwaukee tracks moving at a pretty good clip. All I saw was his back…

1943

Country Religion

When I was growing up on the farm, observance of Sunday as a day of rest was required. It was a day of respite from all but necessary chores, such as feeding animals and making sure the water tanks were not frozen in the winter. We were Lutherans, and my mother was prone to expressing her faith at home. She would play the piano and sing songs like *The Old Rugged Cross* and other good old hymns. Usually on Sunday, we would drive to town to attend church. Of course, that depended on the car starting, the roads being passable, and Dad being home from work. My mother never drove a car during her lifetime.

It felt good to head to town…

Getting everything ready and in place so we could attend church was a fiasco. We had to get scrubbed in an old washtub and put on clean clothes—cramming our feet into stiff, confining shoes was a real chore. But, once ready to go, it felt good to be heading into town with a chance to see old friends and lie about everything if you wanted to. Since we never lied about people, we didn't consider the fact that we were "bearing false witness." The second best part was to watch all the girls in their pretty dresses and cute shoes, usually with pigtails of blonde or dark hair. The last thing we did was to file into church accompanied by organ music—loud, ongoing, and a little foreboding.

All of the kids under the age of 13 had to sit in the front pew to the left of the preacher. I didn't connect "minister" with the term "preacher" until I was ten. I somehow thought that the minister was a man who ministered to people if they became ill in church. The preacher's name was Eldon, and he was older and somewhat crotchety. When everyone was seated, the preacher would enter the church and walk slowly towards the podium, carrying the Bible in his left hand against his chest. This was a ritual that never changed as long as I attended church. He would stop at the podium and raise his hands up, and we would all stand and sing the opening song. Then he would begin to preach.

When he began, his voice was normal, but as he progressed, his voice got louder and louder. And he would sometimes hit the podium with the flat of his hand to emphasize a point. He would glare at us kids as he was preaching. We were all sitting so quiet you could hear a mouse walk. He scared Fats and me every time. Most Sundays were well organized, and after the sermon, all of the kids would attend Sunday school. That portion of the service was usually held in little rooms for various age groups and was a fun time... that is, until one Sunday night after Christmas 1941.

The frog was tame, but just wasn't used to church...

The war had begun, and the church was almost over-crowded with parents who had kids draft age. Everyone was solemn and attentive to the words of the preacher. My friend Fats and I usually sat together in the first pew. On this particular Sunday, Fats had come to church in bib overalls with a chest pocket that bulged out in front and that looked like it held a bandana. During the latter part of the sermon, Fats confided in me that he had a little green frog in his pocket in a damp handkerchief. He had played with it all summer, and it was tame. He planned to bring it to school all winter to play with. He reached into the bib pocket, pulled out the red bandana, and held it down between our legs.

Carefully removing the frog from the bandana, he held it behind its front legs, and it was perfectly still. It was green with black spots and looked like it had the measles. Fats held it for a few minutes and then started to put the frog back into the bandana. About that time, the preacher hit the podium with his fist real hard, and the frog jumped out of Fats' hand and onto the floor. All of the kids in the front row saw it happen and started to snicker. Fats made a grab for the frog but it jumped away, and Fats fell out of his seat, rolled toward the altar, and knocked over a candle stand, breaking the candle. He must have momentarily forgot where he was, as he said, "Oh, sh**!" And in the process of getting to his feet, he stepped on the rear end of the frog. He didn't hurt the frog, though, who then hopped across the aisle and onto an elderly lady's leg. She had seen it coming at her and let out a scream while her husband tried to grab it. He fell out of his seat and kicked the other candleholder over, breaking it and the candle. Fats went to help the elderly gentleman up, but he pushed Fats away with his foot. Fats fell onto the lap of one of the young ladies, who screamed and pushed him onto the floor.

All this time, I was sitting in the pew, holding onto the seat. It all happened so fast that no one moved. The preacher was standing at the podium wringing his hands. Someone in the second row caught the frog. When the preacher saw the frog was caught, he looked up and said, "Amen."

The aftermath of this fiasco was that Fats' dad had to buy two new long white candles and repair the candleholder, and Fats had to apologize to the congregation, memorize *John 3:16,* and recite it the next Sunday. He was also forbidden to sit in the front row for two Sundays. The man who fell on the floor told Fats' dad that all Fats needed was a good thrashing. He later told Fats' dad that his wife had nightmares of being eaten by green bugs with red eyes and spots.

We became the best kids in the front row...

The next time we attended church, Fats sat by me again and asked me if I wanted a chew. I declined, and that was the last time he wore bib overalls to church. He also remarked that, when the collection plate was passed, he always wanted to take some change out, but he was afraid he would get caught. And I'm sure he would have.

Every Sunday after that, the preacher always looked right at Fats and me when he would smack the podium and say that all unforgiven sinners would surely rest in Hell. I didn't know what I had done, but I wasn't taking any chances, and Fats and I became the most attentive kids in the front row.

1942

Curly Franks

One morning in early August of 1942, I was cleaning up our garden area, pulling up dead vines, and collecting cucumbers and tomatoes so they could be put up for use all winter. In Floyd County, Iowa, everyone seemed to have a garden, and it was a Godsend to have vegetables all winter. We always had a whole passel of beans, carrots, cucumbers, tomatoes, beets, and cabbage to increase the variety of food when the snow was on the ground. Most of our neighbors would trade back and forth, so we had access to more items than the farmers' market. After about an hour, I had denuded the garden of all the leftover debris and was leaning on the front fence by the gate trying to cool off. I looked up the road, and I could see a man peddling a bicycle towards our farm. In a few seconds, he pulled an old Schwinn bicycle through the gate and jumped off, resting the machine on the fence. Tied on a sort of carrier over the back fender was a huge box, which contained one whale of a bunch of something.

Names sure can be deceiving...

The man who hopped off the bicycle was an older man, about 60 years old I thought, and he greeted me with, "Hello, young feller, it looks like we've been blessed with a beautiful summer day."

I looked at him and said, "Yup, sure is."

He looked over the garden spot and said, "Clearing off the garden, huh?"

I said, "Yup, getting rid of all the debris so I won't have to do it next spring." I was only 13 years old, but I was some taller than he was.

He had an old straw hat on his head that had a string tied to the brim in case of wind, and the front of the brim was turned up and really dirty on the right side. The front peak had a good-sized hole in it, and when he saw me looking at it, he said, "That hole lets the air in to cool my head in the heat."

He stuck out his hand and said, "My name's Curly Franks, and I used to be a blacksmith until I retired. Now I mainly put new shoes on horses for a small fee and a meal or two. I've ridden that two-wheeled scooter all the way from St. Paul, Minnesota, and I have to take a day or two off." He had on a blue denim shirt with one side torn about halfway down, and his jeans were clean, but torn some around the cuffs.

As I was looking him over, he was looking at our two saddle horses standing by the stock tank in the shade. I kept looking at his hat, expecting him to remove his straw hat and expose a full head of grey hair. I just assumed that anyone named "Curly" would have curly hair on his head. Boy, was I wrong—he reached up and pulled the hat off, and he was as bald as an egg with no shell. His face was free of wrinkles and looked tighter than the skin on a grape. Curly turned, looked at me, and said, "Are those the only horses you own?" I told him that we also had two workhorses that did most of the farming. I also told him that the riding horses had a couple of the loose shoes. He hesitated for a minute or two and then asked me if my dad was anywhere around so he could talk about putting new iron on the two saddle horses. I told Curly that Dad would be home before too long and that I was pretty sure he would be receptive to having Curly work on the horses.

Looking around, he spied our Do-All Rumely tractor, and he said it was one of the best machines ever built.

Everything he owned fit in the box on the back of his bike...

Then he asked me if he could sleep down by the corncrib until morning. He had everything he needed in his traveling box on the bicycle. I told him it would be okay, and if he needed water, to help himself to the pump, but to stay away from the other buildings. I watched as he opened the box and took out a bedroll, coffee pot, and a small sack of food. I followed as he pushed the bicycle over to the shed. He pulled out the biggest gunnysack I had ever seen. He smiled and said, "Everything I own follows me around on this bike. I just wish it would help me peddle once in a while." I told him, if it rained, to use the granary for shelter. He laid out his bedroll and then went to the pump and filled up an old porcelain coffee pot with water. Curly built a small fire and hung the coffee pot next to the fire on a stick. After he drank some coffee, he laid down on his bedroll, removed his hat, and closed his eyes.

When my brother Ed came driving into the yard, he asked me what was with the man on the blanket—was he dead or something? I told him what was happening, and Ed just shook his head and went into the house. Dad came home later, and I filled him in too. Dad didn't appear upset; he just asked me if Curly had wanted to shoe all four horses. I told him that Curly hadn't said.

Handling horses can be tricky...

In the morning, Dad hired Curly to shoe both riding horses but said to leave the big Belgiums alone. Dad told him where to find the gear and shoes for the horses. Dad told me later that Curly was a sort of a blacksmith and that I was to treat him like company. He invited Curly to have dinner with us and partake of a good breakfast before he left in the morning. He gave Curly the $10 he asked for and told him to sleep in the bunkhouse at night. Dad also told Mother to fix him a good sack lunch when he left the farm.

Ed and I were just finishing the milking when Curly stuck his head in the barn door and asked me if I would help him by handing him the tools when he started to shoe our two riding horses. I told him I'd be glad to help. I watched as he led Star, our oldest horse, out of the barn and tied him to the hitching post. Curly seemed to have a way with horses, and when he lifted up Star's left front leg, the horse never moved. Curly "broke the leg" so that the bottom of the hoof faced upward. He felt the worn-out shoe he was going to replace. "Hey, Sonny," he said to me, "hand me the end nippers; that shoe is so loose I'm going to get it off."

Curly pulled out the nails on the shoe and said, "It's funny that piece of iron didn't fall off long ago." I could see that it was worn down to nothing. Curly removed the nails, came over, and sat down beside me. He said, "I'm here to tell you that that horse has breath so bad it'd melt all the paint off the chicken coop. He must have a snoot full of rotten teeth." He reached into his hip pocket, pulled out a small piece of plug chewing tobacco, and offered it to me. I shook my head, and he bit off a small piece of tobacco and worried it into his cheek. Then he got up, picked up a new shoe, and went back to Star. I never did see him spit.

After finishing with Star, Curly started shoeing Blackie, our other riding horse. Blackie kept turning his head to watch what Curly was doing, like he didn't trust him. All the time Curly was using the file and fitting the shoes on Blackie, the horse acted worried. Curly handed me the platers rasp he had in his pocket. Then he suddenly let out a string of nasty words aimed at "that big, black, good for nothing, s.o.b., who was only good enough to be ground up for dog food!" Curly hobbled over to a block of wood and sat down, took off his shoe and sock, and rubbed his sore foot.

Curly looked at me and said, "That coyote-bait kicked me on the ankle and stepped on my foot. I think it's broken." I pumped a bucket full of cold water and had him soak his foot for quite a while. The foot was bruised, but not broken, and two of his toes looked like ripe purple grapes with bloody glasses on. I was plumb glad he had finished shoeing Blackie before getting kicked. I spotted Ed looking out the barn window, and he was laughing. Curly hopped on one foot towards the bunkhouse, followed by our big, grey goose. I think he figured that the goose was going to attack him too.

Three days and he was gone again...

Monday morning came on early, and when I got up, Curly was sitting on the front porch, all dressed with both shoes on. Curly told me, as he was getting ready to ride away on his bike, that Blackie also had breath so bad that, when he breathed out, it almost singed his hair. He told me that bad breath was a sign of bad teeth and that the horse probably had every animal disease in the vet's book. I never told Curly that Ed was always feeding both horses sugar cubes, string tobacco, and used-up mash from one of his friend's whiskey stills.

Mother brought out a good-sized flour sack about half full of sandwiches, fruit, and cookies. Curly thanked Mom for the sack of food, bit off a chunk of plug tobacco, swung a leg over the bicycle, and peddled off down the road. He had only been around for three days, but I hated to see him go. I had never encountered anyone like him before, and I knew that he had a million stories to tell. I checked out the bunkhouse, and he had left it clean and neat. I found a token good for five cents in trade at Knox's Pool Hall. The only problem was that Knox's Pool Hall was in Cedar Falls, Iowa — one heck of a long ways from our farm.

1943

Ed and the Boar Hog, Lucifer

While growing up on our Floyd County farm, 1938 was a learning year for me: some new cuss words, a lesson about fencing hogs apart from each other, and information about a new bout with a bug similar to Cow Pox. By George, it forecast a summer that would be almost too busy to enjoy. It all began in May just before school adjourned for the summer.

Becoming a wealthy farmer wasn't easy...

Ed was my older brother — three and a half long years older — who was continuously trying to teach me to be a successful farmer, a horse jockey, a dairy cow specialist, a hog farmer, and a dead shot with his .22 special rifle. I was only nine years old, coming up to the last week in August. Ed told me that he would teach me to become a wealthy farmer between chores. Somehow, I just didn't believe him, because he sure as heck wasn't loaded down with money and always tried to borrow *my* allowance. He must have needed money because he had five girlfriends and a 1931 Chevrolet Sedan that always needed expensive fixin'.

Ed Anderson. 15 years old. 1940.

My education this summer would be hands-on participation of technical chores that only an educated man, dedicated and sincerely interested in becoming a first-class wealthy farmer, would undertake. At least, that was what Ed imparted to me. I agreed to the requirements because, if I didn't, I figured I would face a bunch of mental abuse and some unpleasant physical contact and be treated like an outcast by Ed and his friends. Granted, his buddies were not farmers; some were borderline good citizens, and a few were constantly checked on by the truant officer, but I figured that, if I was to learn anything, I'd have to cooperate with Ed and do whatever he asked me to do.

I dreaded the coming of summer and all Ed's teaching because I liked to be able to spend a few hours doing nothing, except for my chores. I loved to spend time with my friend Fats and his dog, Carson. It was fun to sit on our back porch and hope that one of Ed's girlfriends would come to see my mother and that I'd get the chance to visit with her. All of Ed's girlfriends were good-looking and always smelled like fresh flowers. I wanted to be around to see the salesmen that came by every summer to get us to buy whatever they were selling because, according to them, it would be impossible to survive if we didn't. I also wanted to be free to follow the Revenuers and County Sheriff as they snooped around all the farms trying to find the illegal corn-cooking stills. And finally, I wanted to go to town with any of my friends that might come by to see the Saturday Westerns.

I listed these all out and then give the list to Ed. I hoped to influence him to be kind and not work me into an old man, unable to enjoy all the things I liked to do. Ed took the list and read it as we walked towards the barn. He never said a word and did not even smile. He folded up my list and put it into his shirt pocket. I found the list later in our manure spreader laying on top of a full load of nutrients from the cow stalls waiting to be spread all over the pasture. Sadly, I knew then that I was going to benefit from Ed's lessons, learn how to be a rich famer, learn more dirty tricks, and add to my forbidden vocabulary—like it or not.

Curing the Seven-Year-Itch...

The first Saturday after the school locked up its doors, my friend Fats came into my yard with Carson slinking along behind, looking like he had been forbidden to be happy. We visited for a while, talking about coming events and our plans for all of our free time. Then, out of nowhere, Fats said that he had a new disease called the Seven-Year-Itch. He said that his dad had got the dad-burn disease a year ago, and all his dad did was scratch, chew tobacco, and spit a lot. His ma bought his dad a watch for Christmas. It was a good-looking thing, and all Fats' dad did was sit around, drink coffee, wind up the watch, and go to the outdoor toilet a whole bunch of times. He spent hours in the machine shop making a scratch stick so he could scratch his back. He put some graphite paste on the business end of the stick and spent quite a bit of time scratching his back. The itch just wouldn't go away, so he went into town and had the doctor look at the sores. Fats said that, when he came home, he had a couple of little tins that were full of sulphur in something that looked like brown-colored hog fat. He said that the doctor told his dad that he had something called scabies that he had to treat it or it wouldn't go away, and that it was a highly contagious affliction. At the first sign of any member of his family starting to itch, the doctor said to smear a big glob of salve on the spot. Fats' dad had to cover his whole body with the salve and stay in bed one full day, covered up so he would sweat, and that would cure the disease.

Fats told me that the salve cured the itching and that his mom had to boil all of his dad's clothes in a big pot and then wash them in lye water. This conversation really got to me, and I scooted away from Fats. I had lived through a bout of cowpox, and it seemed to be a first cousin to this new thing called scabies. So, after Fats left to go home, I took a dip in the horse tank and put on clean clothes, just to be safe. I was sitting in the sun on the back porch when Ed came home and sat down to talk with me about the summer.

Lucifer was meaner than a rabid bulldog…

We talked a while, and then Ed said, "Find an old pair of Dad's leather gloves and get an old pair of sunglasses from Mom. We're about to fix a fence across the pig pen to keep the old boar away from the new sows Dad bought." Dad had bought a couple of new brides for the old boar, and Dad wanted us to section off the big pen to keep them for a couple of weeks so they could get used to our place. After I finally rounded up the tools needed, I followed Ed out to the pen. Ed showed me the part of the pen we had to isolate. It was the part where the fat, old worthless boar laid around in a good-sized mud bath. Since pigs can't jump like sheep, it would be easy to control a big, fat boar with a short wire fence with a single string of barbwire across the top. Ed called our old boar Lucifer and told me that he was meaner than a rabid bulldog with a thorn in his eye. We drew a line in the dirt, dividing the 30- x 45-foot pen to keep the big, old boar away from his new lady friends. That line cut through part of the boar's mud bath, but Ed figured that he could share one side of the mud bath with his new friends. Ed prodded the boar in the south end with a pitchfork until he went to the far end of the pen and lay down. We had a roll of hog wire, and we nailed it to the barn and across the pen to the fence. The new area for the boar was 10- x 20-feet with the divider about four feet tall.

Ed checked the outside wooden fence, and he said we would add several new posts to make sure Lucifer didn't break the fence out when we turned the new girls loose. We finally finished the job, and Ed told me that there was no way the boar could get through the fence to eat any baby pigs. Ed told me to open the newly gated area so we could turn the boar out to drink silage juice and root around in the spilled silage. That brown puddle around our silo smelled with the odor of corn squeezin's, and I figured that our animals were all drunks.

Ed was as nervous as a new bride...

Ed was as brave as they come, self-proclaimed to be the smartest, handsomest, toughest man on our county road. I had thought on that once, and there were only four farms on our stretch of graveled road. And not counting Dad, there only three other men in the area to be tougher than, and all three were old men... But I humored Ed and told him that, as far as I knew, he was absolutely right. That included men and beasts, and if I figured right, as long as the boar was in pen, Ed didn't have to prove a darn thing. But if the boar got out of the pen, it would probably make Ed the fastest runner in Floyd County. Old Lucifer was not domesticated one iota. And I was scared of his big fang-like teeth that were at least four inches long and looked like white spikes sticking out of his bottom jaw. Besides, he weighed over 250 pounds and grunted all the time, even when he was laying in his mud bath. One of our young sows had the name of Miss Bette, pasted on her by the former owner's wife. Ed told me that the pig had pretty blue eyes like Bette Davis. Whenever I went with Ed to feed the pigs, I watched Bette while she watched Ed, blinked her eyes, and never moved until Ed left the area. That fascinated me, but when I told Mom about it, all she said was that Bette didn't trust Ed because he always carried a pitchfork. I figured that had to be right, as pigs didn't trust humans much.

As Ed was attaching the hog fence to the barn, the boar stood about ten feet away, watching Ed and grunting with every breath. Ed dropped his hammer, and I picked it up to hand to Ed. As I handed the hammer to Ed over his shoulder, it was so slippery that I dropped it, and it hit Ed's shoulder. Ed jumped up and away from the barn, slipping in the mud and falling backwards at the boar. The slip scared the pig, and it made a fast retreat to the far end of the pen. All Ed could see was the boar running at him and grunting with every gasp. He sounded like a fat man trying to tie his shoes. Ed ended up with mud all over his pants. After a few minutes, he smelled worse than an outhouse in July, called the boar a few new words I hadn't heard before, and went to the house to clean up. I'm sure the boar figured that Ed was going to attack him, and Ed figured the boar was going to chew off a little skin. And Ed probably figured he was in for retribution for past abuse of the animal.

When Ed came back, he was pretty shaken up, and when we finished the pen, he was as nervous as a new bride. He told me he was lucky the boar had just eaten, or it might have bitten off a leg or arm. He had just fed Lucifer a five-gallon pail of slop. Lucifer always ate everything he could find, including the apples Ed tossed to him every day, and pushed the sows aside to eat their food if he could. His diet consisted of five gallons twice a day, skim milk filled with peelings and old bread, as well as lots of apples that fell from our trees. That day, Ed told me that the old boar was gonna be bacon, lard, and ham come October. I told Ed that any food we got out of him to eat would be like trying to eat the horses' harness—hames and all.

That episode must have scared Ed pretty bad, because he left me alone until September when he recruited me to help trap varmints. Ed stayed completely away from the pigpen, and when September rolled around, we loaded Lucifer into the butcher's pickup, and he took his final ride to the butcher shop. The big thing that I thought about was that Ed was a brave brother, but big boar hogs were a whole lot tougher.

1939

Farm Life

Ed's project before we started back to school was a dandy and worth repeating to all red-blooded young men. He confided in me that he had thought of a way to kill all of the flies around our barn. There were zillions of the little buggers hated by humans and animals alike. Killing them would be an achievement worth millions, and he had my complete attention. He started to explain the eradication plan that he said was foolproof and guaranteed to work. He said that we would split the fortune 50—50 and even market the idea in Europe; that alone should have raised a red flag, but it didn't, and I listened to his idea.

Ed said we were going to raise wasps and make a million...

Our barn, like barns all over the area, was loaded with flies. Our barn also had several hundred little grey nests that hung from the rafters like sunflowers. There was a mixture of pods to accommodate the wasps, hornets, yellow jackets, and quite a few others I didn't know. No one had ever bothered those nests for two reasons: the darn things all had stingers and besides those rafters were 40 feet high. No one had ever been stung on our farm; everyone ignored them, and they ignored us. Ed's thoroughly thought out idea was to take down all of those nests and clean them out. Then we would glue them to several long boards in the lower level of the barn so we would reach them. He talked, and I listened. By being able to reach the nests, we could control the quantity of nests to be used and regulate the occupants as to size.

We would discourage the smaller ones and cover up their hives. When the new tenants arrived in the spring, we would cover all the nests except those we wanted to fill, uncovering more as needed. When the pods all filled up with larva, we would harvest them and lay them in our chick incubator to mature. As they came out of their nests, we would feed them sugar water and make them think we were their keepers. As they grew, we would catch lots of flies and put them in with the wasps. They would learn to like the taste of the flies and would dine on them instead of the sugar water. Also, they would hang around us all the time, and we would teach them all kinds of tricks and maybe sell a few to the circus.

I asked Ed what the wasps would eat once the flies were all gone, but he didn't answer... We went to work and moved about 20 of the biggest pods, some of which were a foot across. We glued them to a long board and quit for the day. The next morning we were up early, and Ed started to knock down a few more. He knocked down a big one, and all of a sudden, I heard him yell, "Run for your life! They're attacking us!" He had loosened one that was already full, and there were about 100 of those darn things coming at Ed. I was only stung twice but Ed really got the brunt of that attack.

For some reason, I almost looked forward to school again...

After Ed got out of the hospital, he came home to get ready for school. I didn't recognize him right off as he looked like one great big pimple. His head and arms were dotted similar to a bad case of the chicken pox. He also had bumps on his head the size of hazelnuts. He just loafed around, and it took a few days for the stings to recede. Actually, he looked like a derelict from a sideshow with the worst case of acne in the world. When Dad came home, he destroyed all of the nests after lecturing Ed again. I almost looked forward to school again, as Ed would be living in town and I would be by myself.

1946

Gold Coins and Liberty Bonds

During 1938, as the starve-to-death-days of the Depression started to relax their hold on the economy, times weren't as bad as they had been in 1937. It seems to me that everybody had relaxed some, and more people would be in town on Saturdays. Farmers had a bit more money, and most of them bought more items for the kitchen and non-essential items for the family. Most of the farmers in our area of the county purchased all of their food supplies at a store named "The Farmers Cash Market." It was a good-sized store, and besides groceries and produce, they sold items like fishing tackle, rubber boots, gloves, and an assortment of coveralls and jackets. Charles City was a small town, and the local people really supported local businesses. The loyalty arose from the fact that The Farmers Cash Market purchased vegetables from all of the farmers that had extra items for sale and paid a fair price in cash. Proceeds from these sales were not considered income, and in most cases, wives spent the few dollars very frugally.

I had been totally, fatally in love with nine ladies...

I always looked forward to these Saturday shopping trips, especially because one of the clerks in the grocery store was a young, red-haired girl with green eyes. She was always pleasant, and in my estimation, prettier than a clear September sunset. Unless I forgot a few of Ed's girlfriends, I had been totally, fatally in love with nine ladies, and that didn't include a couple of school teachers, a Sunday School teacher, two ladies who worked for our doctor, and a little blonde named Mary Jane Carr, who was in the third grade.

Every other Saturday, Dad would take the whole family to town to buy needed items and take on the town. Mother would spend an hour or more looking at fabrics and buying a few necessities. Then we would spend some time at the farmers' market, visiting with other farmers and picking out the most needed food items we couldn't grow, such as coffee, salt, sugar, and flour. I would just stand by and keep my attention on the red-haired clerk. Dad had quite a few liberty bonds he had saved. The Roosevelt recall of all gold came, but Dad had a batch of gold coins he didn't turn in. He kept them in a tobacco tin in the barn, and he always said he was going to take them to the bank. Whenever we went to town, Dad would always take a handful of bonds and trade them at the grocery store for about half of their face value. I watched one Saturday when he gave the storeowner four of the Liberty Bonds for the groceries that we took home. The grocer was happy to get them, and Dad was plumb tickled to get rid of them. Dad told me that the grocer was smarter and slicker than the banker and would make a good profit on the exchange. The grocer's name was Silverman and at one time had been a junk dealer.

He was as ugly as seven miles of gumbo road...

One Saturday I went with Dad, and he bought a five-gallon pail of oil for our equipment and gave the owner of the garage two gold coins as payment. The coins were about the size of a five-cent coin and shiny yellow. Dad also had some coins with an Indian head and some with a woman's head that had "Liberty" on her headband. He told me that they were worth five dollars each, but he couldn't spend them. He later gave me two of each and told me to save them.

It seemed to me that every time Dad would drive our big Buick down to the garage, one of the mechanics would walk up and visit with us. He always talked about the hard times and how hard it was to just-get-by. He always watched as Dad paid the garage with gold coins, which were taken right to the owner. I had the feeling that that mechanic would take some of Dad's coins if he had the opportunity. He was not married, and he was ugly as seven miles of gumbo road.

Another Saturday, my brother Ed went to town with us, and Dad said he had to pick up some oil for our old oil pull Do-All Rumely tractor. We drove down to the Buick garage, and Dad ordered the oil. The pest of a mechanic saw us waiting for the oil, and he came scurrying from the back of the garage to see Dad. He was watching when Dad gave the parts man two gold coins for the oil. When we entered our car to leave, he asked Dad where in the devil he was getting the gold coins. Dad told him that he had forgot to turn them in when the government called them in. Then the mechanic asked Dad something about the big exhibition that was coming to town the next Saturday and would last all day. Ed was sitting in the front seat, and I figured that he had heard what was said and would tell me later. After that trip, I never saw that mechanic again, and I didn't figure that I was missing anything.

Something erupted from his backpack...

The big exhibition was always held at the airport, far enough away from the hard-packed landing road so the planes could come and go. The organizers lined up all the new cars, all the new farm equipment, and both new and old tractors. There were several aeroplanes with two wings that were listed as bi-planes, and they were kept flying almost all day. The Grand Air finally started just before dark. One of the planes took off, circled the area for a bit, and then suddenly turned all the way over so that a man fell out of the back seat. We watched him fall, and we all knew that he would certainly perish when he hit the ground. When he was not very far above the ground, something erupted from his backpack! It was a big, white parachute, and he floated safely down. Everybody there yelled, shouted, clapped their hands, and yelled, creating a real loud noise. Ed said, "Those poor idiots should have known that the bosses wouldn't let anyone deliberately jump out of an aeroplane and kill himself." An awful lot of people were thankful as the dickens that the parachute opened in time.

After that nerve-wracking stunt, the exhibiters fired up several of the old, smoke-belching behemoths that ran on wood and paraded them all around the field. They even had a tractor pull to see which steamer could pull the best. The one that won all the honors was a great big Rumely that pulled two of the smaller ones backward at the same time as they were spinning their wheels to go forward.

Folks from other communities also came to the exhibition, and that was a sure sign that our area was getting better right along. We attended as a family and spent the whole day until just about dark, climbing on tractors and sitting in all the new cars.

The house was ransacked…

It was pushing real dark when we arrived home, and we still had the chores to do before supper. My mother went into the house to start supper, and as Dad was locking up the car, Mom came hurrying out of the house. I heard her tell Dad that someone had pried open the kitchen door and ransacked the house. I asked for details, and she told me that someone had broken into the house and dumped all of the dresser drawers out onto the kitchen floor.

Dad came into the house, looked at the huge pile of clothing on the kitchen floor, and went to get the sheriff. We only lived five miles from town, and Dad returned, followed by a deputy sheriff, in about ten minutes. The deputy looked all through the house and asked us if we could tell what was missing. Mother said it looked like whoever broke in was looking for money because nothing was broken up. She also told him that we kept no money in the house and that all of the decorations were still intact. I helped clean up the mess, and just as we were finishing, my brother Ed came driving up from town. When he found out what had happened, he said, "I'll bet I know who did the break-in." He turned to me and said, "Remember that idiot mechanic at the garage who watched Dad pay for the oil with gold coins?" I said I remembered, and Ed said, "I'll bet he figured that Dad had a bunch of money hidden in the house because Dad was never out of work and had a steady income all the time." Ed went out to the barn and told Dad what he thought.

Rough justice…

When Ed left for school the next day, he told me that he was going to do some sleuthing on his own. Ed was 15 years old but looked older. He was over six feet tall, all muscle, and I knew he had never been beaten in a fight. He could ride the fur right off any horse or bull and tan the hide in the process.

The week went by slowly, and Ed was gone most of the time until Friday. The deputy sheriff pulled into the yard with Ed right behind him. The deputy and Ed left right away in the sheriff's blue car. A few hours later, they came back, and Ed came into the house and told us that they had solved the break-in and that it was, indeed, the mechanic named Baldwin, who was currently residing in a cell, booked for burglary. Ed told me later that the mechanic had asked Dad if he ever took the family to the big doin's at the airport, and Ed had heard Dad say, "You bet. We go as a family and spend the whole day there." According to Ed, that was the break in the case. The deputy remarked that the crook had cried like a baby and carried on like a newly made steer when he was caught. Dad told Ed to watch his back for the next few weeks.

School started the first week of September in 1938, and I was now a fourth grader. One of the Kelloge kids told our teacher that someone had really beat up Baldwin and that he had his right arm in a sling. I figured that he had accosted Ed, and Ed had beat the whey out of him. Later, Ed told me that the jackass had come at him with a baseball bat and that Ed took it away from him. Ed told me that, when he walked away, the crook was laying on the ground so Ed kept the bat. The deputy told Ed that he didn't think there would be any more trouble.

I was barely ten years old; this was the most unforgettable event that happened on our farm. Dad didn't have to attend the short trial, but he told me he had broken the law by not turning in the gold. Dad later turned the rest of the coins in at the bank except for some he gave to Ed and me. We found out later that the crook left the area, and we never saw him again. All the rest of the Liberty Bonds were traded for groceries. Later Dad traded in our 1934 Buick and bought a new white car that was great. It was a 1939 Buick. Ed still picked up girls in his old 1931 Chevy.

1942

Gus' Parachute

One day in March of 1937, not long after Gus Miller had the bad accident trying to fly the homemade, single-wing airplane that he and his dad had made (that wouldn't fly), I went over to see how he was getting along. He lived right across the county road from our farm with his mom Nola, his dad Art, and a whole passel of all-American dogs that barked all of the time. Gus was just getting healed up from a broken leg from the crash of the handmade plane that he tried to fly off their barn roof. I had visited with him a few times and always got a big piece of apple pie that just slid down without chewing and a glass of chocolate milk. His mother never said much, and she always seemed to be as nervous as a 20-year smoker trying to quit tobacco. All Gus did was lie in bed and complain about everything. Old Man Miller, as he was known, never said too much about the accident, but he read and re-read all of his books about airplanes.

Some folks just never learn...

I was ending the fourth grade, and Gus was in the seventh grade, hoping to get into the eighth grade so he could get out of school and become a fighter pilot. Our teacher, Miss Heise, was doing her best to get him through school, and she helped Gus a lot with his studies. He didn't like book learning, but he loved anything to do with aviation, and that was about all he talked about. Gus kept one of his dad's airplane books in his room, and he read and re-read it continuously and knew quite a bit about flying. That book was full of pictures of county fairs and the participation of pilots with airplanes in quite a few of those fairs. It showed bi-planes; monoplanes; one three-winged plane called a Fokker doing all kinds of diving, rolling, and looping; and even someone with a parachute strapped on jumping out of a bi-plane. Gus and I visited about the pictures, and that was when he told me that he was going to get a job with the air circus when he got his cast off. He told me that the doctor that had just been out to see him had told him that he might remove the cast in about one week. The only stipulation was that Gus would have use crutches for a while to get used to walking again.

When I left him to go home, Gus mentioned that a pilot named Rider was the one who had jumped out of an airplane and was a war hero. (Actually, the pilot's name was Rideout, and he later died in an airplane crash.) I thought about Gus for a while, and I went back to see him the following week. Lo and behold, he was sitting at the table eating a bowl of soup, and he was as chipper as a grey squirrel in an acorn tree. His first question was if I thought a big umbrella would enable him to jump off the barn roof and land safely on the ground. I knew that the barn was 60 feet high, but he was as serious as a fox after a fat hen, and I just couldn't answer the question. I told him that I would ask the extension agent about that when I went to town and would come back when I had the information. The next Saturday, I went to town with Dad. I stopped at the extension office and asked the agent if an umbrella could be used as a parachute to jump off a barn and not get hurt.

The agent looked at me as if I had said I was going to commit Hari-Kari, shook his head, and asked me if I was going to try it. He said that, if I was, he just hoped the roof was only a foot or two off the ground. He explained the reason that it wouldn't work was that the umbrella was made to shed water and not hold air. It was made of real thin metal ribs to hold it open, and if you tried to use it to stop a fall, it would collapse outward and break all of the stays. There were no holes in the top to let some of the air pressure out, and even if there had been some holes, that wouldn't make any difference. Besides that, a parachute did not have stays to keep it open; it opened up when it was released from its container, and it needed several hundred feet to do that. I didn't understand all of what he said, but I figured that, if Gus jumped off the barn roof, he would break both legs—maybe every bone in his body.

Gus was as serious as a young bull in a herd of heifers...

The agent sent me over to the library to get information on anything to do with airplanes. They had quite a few brochures and a booklet or two, and I checked out the ones I thought Gus would like. One of them had an article about a man named Rickenbacker, who was a good pilot. The next day I took the information over to Gus, and he was really glad to get it. We looked over the brochures; one showed a man with a parachute strapped on, rolling out of a plane that was almost upside down. The pilot was in the front seat with a leather cap and goggles on. When I left to go home, Gus told me he was going to make a big parachute out of canvas and jump off his barn. He said that fighter pilots sometimes were shot down, and he figured he could parachute if he was shot down. Besides that, he said that the crash he had went through had hurt like hell, and he didn't want to be laid up in some hospital overseas during any war we got into. Old Man Miller was listening to Gus, and he remarked that there would never be another war because (President) Coolidge had said so.

Almost a month later, Gus was walking around with crutches and sitting on the porch drawing pictures of parachutes and planes. He had also acquired several old black umbrellas and had them stacked on the porch open for rain. I visited with him for a while and asked him if he was really serious about learning how to fly. He said he was as serious as a young bull in a herd of heifers. He had tied a rock to one of the umbrellas and had thrown it off the chicken coop, and it had floated down slowly. He figured that he weighed three times what the rock weighed, so an umbrella three times as big would let him down slowly off the 60-foot barn roof. He said it would be too hard to hang onto three umbrellas, but one giant one would enable him to jump safely. He also said that, if he was right, he would take it up to the 100-foot bluff by the river where it would really work good.

Lath slats, baling wire, rope, and an old canvas tent ...

Gus' dad, Art, never did say much to me any of the times I went over to see Gus. My brother Ed called him a "flash in the pan." I asked Mom what that meant, and she said to look around the attic for Dad's old muzzleloader. She explained that there was a spoon-shaped lid called a frizzed that was placed over the powder charge on the side of the fire hole, which was called the powder pan. When the fire hole got plugged up, the hammer of the gun would fall when pulled, and the flint would ignite the powder in the pan. That explosion would blow the frizzed back up, but the powder in the barrel would not ignite, and the gun would not fire. I spent an hour looking at the humongous Belgium gun, and I finally figured out that Ed meant Art was a blowhard with no action. Later on, Dad explained that Gus was doing what Art wanted to do but couldn't. Gus' dad never commented on the parachute experiment involving Gus, but he didn't counsel against it either. I thought that, if it did work, Art would take all the credit and walk around with his thumbs hooked on his bib overalls, telling everyone that he had figured it all out. And Gus would be as content as a cat with a bowl full of fresh milk for a day or two. Everyone knew that Gus was hurt pretty bad in that accident brought about by his dad's obsession with airplanes.

When I left to go home, I told Gus that he should wait until he was out of school before he jumped off the barn roof. Later on that fall, I went to see Gus, and he was totally healed up. He had spent the entire summer working with a parachute he had fabricated out of lath slats, baling wire, rope, and an old canvas tent. It somewhat resembled a parachute, but looked more like an umbrella or a wool stocking cap that would fit an elephant. He had put 21 lath slats together in seven sticks of three—glued end to end. To brace them, he had overlapped three inches and wrapped baling wire around each joint. He ended up with seven slats, and he used these for the ribs. He nailed and glued the canvas to form a large round wheel, the center drilled out, and a four-inch rod with a ring held them all together. I had to admit that Gus had a lot of engineering ability, but in design only—not practicality.

He stood the contraption on end and bent the slats until the wheel looked like a bowl and then tied a rope across the slats to hold it into shape. He hung a rope from the top center eyebolt down about two feet below the edge of the bowl. He was going to hang onto the rope when he jumped. I looked the darn thing over and went home. I just knew that, if he jumped off the barn holding that rope, he'd probably break his legs or his neck, and I didn't want to be a part of another accident. I told Dad about the parachute, and he just grinned and told me that a lot of people do idiotic things like that. He told me I probably should stay clear of the whole mess. He also said that the Miller family needed more changes in their life style than a two-week newborn with the scours, if they expected a long life.

I thought he was loony, but agreed to help...

The next Sunday, I went over to see Gus, and he was perky as a new colt. He had pulled the parachute up to the roof peak and asked if I would climb up there with him and help throw the chute off the barn when he jumped. I thought he was loony, but I agreed to help. We climbed up to the roof peak where the contraption lay on the edge of the roof, ready to be pushed off. I told Gus that the thing couldn't be used in an airplane unless it could be folded up. His reply was he would hinge the stays, and it would collapse into a round bundle. I told him that it probably would fold up all right. Gus had tied a barn door handle to the hold rope, and I knew that Gus was too proud not to jump. He explained that all I had to do was to push the "chute" off the roof as he jumped. The blasted thing wouldn't have to open, as it was already open. I told him that he would probably hit the ground before the chute had time to catch the air. He just looked at me and said, "Get ready and make sure you get it off the roof with me." Gus grabbed the handle and counted, "One, two, three," and then he jumped. Just as he jumped, the chute started to fall sideways instead of flat to catch the air. For a second or two, it caught on the hay door latch, slowing it down. Gus' dad was standing on the ground by the barn door, and the thing fell straight down. The rim hit Old Man Miller on the left foot and broke some of the slats. It also broke his foot across the top and ruined his left boot. Gus hit the ground on both feet, still holding the end of the rope. He never got a scratch because, when the rim of the chute hung up for a second or two, it slowed his downward trip halfway down.

I climbed down, and Gus was helping his dad to the house. I went home and played in the barn until my brother Ed came home. I told him what had happened, and he just stared at me for a moment. Ed said, "You better stay away from Gus; he's missing quite a few marbles." When Dad came home, Ed told him what had happened, and I was forbidden to go over to Miller's any more.

That winter we moved into town, and I never saw Gus again. They sold their farm, and I never found out where they went. Ed said that, if they went where they belonged, no one free would ever see them again.

1943

Harvesting Tree Burls

Iowa was, and still is, farming country where everything planted grows big. Even the families grew big, and the young ladies grew handsome, straight, tall, and able to handle any emergency. I've never heard of any other area growing corn that tops out as high as a bull elephant's eye like it does in Floyd County, Iowa. My older brother often told me never to stand too long in one place in the field because I'd take root and grow a foot.

I have also never seen black walnut and oak trees as big, healthy, and loaded with acorns and walnuts anywhere else I've ever visited. Our farming area had hundreds of black walnut and oak trees, and we used to cut them up for firewood and building boards. Looking back, it was a terrible waste of resources. We just never replanted any trees. Over the years, we had cut down about 20 full-grown oak and walnut trees, leaving the stumps to disintegrate so the areas could be planted in soybeans and corn, but the stumps never seemed to fall apart or get old and turn to dust.

Just a little dynamite in the right place...

Right after the war began in 1941, Dad heard about the value of walnut burls from an engineer in Portland, Oregon. They were importing the burls from Iowa and Missouri and making the most expensive tabletops available. The going price of a finished black walnut table was over $500, and the burls were worth $200 to $300 if there were no splits or separation on the tops of the wood. In those days, that was the equivalent of two months' pay at the Hart-Parr Tractor factory (later the Oliver Corporation).

On many occasions, Dad had used dynamite to lift the burls out of their resting place without damaging them. Then he would cut them up for firewood, using two wedges that looked like a single-bitted axe without the handle. The blade end was wider than the hammer-headed end, and the wedges unscrewed in the middle to expose a hollow area designed to hold black powder. Dad would unscrew the wedge, fill it with powder, insert a capped fuse in the porthole, and screw it back together. After placing it atop the burl, he would light the fuse, and the wedge would split the burl in two so it could be blown out of its resting place. He always drove the wedge into the top of the burl about five inches or so. I had helped split up several of those big burls with my brother and had become proficient in the use of the wedges. One Sunday, my dad left for St. Paul, Minnesota, and told my brother to dig up two stumps in the pasture and trim off all of the roots. He had sold them to a contractor in St. Paul and planned to send them up the following week.

Ed said all burls were right-handed, but don't tell anybody...

On Monday, Ed rounded up several sticks of dynamite and some fuse and told me to come and help. He filled the two wedges with black powder and picked up two shovels, and we headed out to the pasture where the stumps were quietly resting, not bothering anything. It seemed a dirty shame to roust them out of their own place. He told me to get a double-bitted axe and some matches to light the fuses. I was a mite apprehensive—knowing my brother—and I watched him like a hawk. The stumps were about 40 feet apart. My job was to take the shovel and dig all around the burl, cut off all exposed roots, and help Ed light the fuses. After I had finished all the manual labor, Ed said the stump should jump right out into the pasture and not cause any problems. I knew that was a fact, as I had seen my dad lift them out with two sticks of black powder placed on opposite sides of the stump. When Dad set off the powder, the stump would lift up about five feet into the air and always land to the right side of the hole. Dad told me that, even though he cut the fuse shorter on the right side, the stump always turned over to the right. He said he never figured that mystery out.

Ed told me later that the reason for that was that all burls were right-handed, but not to tell anybody he told me.

Ed put the fuses with dynamite caps already on between the two sticks of powder and taped them together. The fuses were about 30 inches long and slow burning, so we had plenty of time to run over behind the water tank that was about 100 feet away. The dynamite was placed as far under the stump as possible, and Ed lit one fuse while I lit the other one. When they started sputtering, we ran over to the water tank and crouched down as far as we could. Ed said, "Prepare yourself for a major earthquake and watch out for falling rocks."

In a few moments, we heard a double "boom," and some clods of dirt fell into the water tank. After a few moments, we got up to see if the stump jumped out okay. Sure as heck, the stump was lying beside the hole, and when the smoke cleared, we had a humongous hole to fill in. The stump looked like a gigantic elephant's tooth with six roots. When we finished filling the hole with rocks and dirt, we trimmed all of the roots off. It was a big stump and must have weighed a few hundred pounds. It looked kind of pitiful, resting there plumb naked. Ed harnessed up the horses, and we threw a log chain around the burl and drug it up to the yard. The Drayage Company would pick it up later in the week. That chore took all day, and we planned to remove the other one the next day.

That night we listened to the news about the war in Europe and heard about a general named Rommel, who was winning victories in the war. Ed had tried to join the Navy, but he was considered necessary to the war effort on the farm and was deferred unless the war turned against us. According to a newscaster named Edward R. Murrow, Britain would never surrender to Hitler. But the Krauts (as Dad called them) appeared to be winning. It really upset my mother, and she remarked that they might conquer the world.

Ed said some other adjectives I didn't really understand...

The next morning Ed and I gathered up the tools and went out to remove the other huge stump. It sat closer to the windmill by our scrap pile, and it was about half the size of the one we had already removed the day before. We cleared away the dirt and roots and placed the dynamite under the stump. It seemed loose, and Ed said all that was holding it down was the taproot. He told me that the root went straight down and secured the tree and sucked up water for the tree. We lit the fuses and ran behind the water tank. After a few seconds, we heard one big explosion, and rocks and dirt rained down, splashing out some of the water. We looked at the stump, and it was still there where it had been all along. We walked over to the stump, and it looked like a permanent fixture, with all of the surrounding dirt missing. Ed surveyed the stump for a few minutes and then fixed two more charges, placed them under the stump, lit the fuse, and we split. When the dynamite went off, the stump went up into the air about ten feet and settled right back into its resting place, like it had never left. Ed walked around the hole a few time and muttered something about its relatives and its sanitary habits and a few other adjectives I didn't really understand. He went over to the barn and returned with the team of horses and a long log chain. We tied the chain around the stump and hooked it to the double tree behind the team. Ed got off to one side and slapped the reins, and the horses pulled the stump right out of the hole. We looked the stump over, and it was ruptured right across the top and good for nothing but firewood. Ed said a few more words over the stump, and we looked around for a different one we could get ready for shipment.

Not all advice is created equal...

We found one on the north side of the barn. We did all of the same preparations and were sitting on the stump eating a sandwich when one of Ed's girlfriends named Marjorie came riding up on her pony to see what we were doing. She was one of his prettiest friends. She had blond hair, blue eyes, and oodles of brown freckles on her cheeks. She lived about three miles away and came to see Mother quite a bit. She looked the stump over and told Ed that the best way to remove it was to put the dirt back into the hole around the stump, pack the dirt down good, and run the fuses up and out of the hole. Ed argued for a few minutes, but after she left, he did what she suggested. Ed moved the horses back to the barn; we lit the fuses and ran back to the barn. After a few minutes, we heard a double explosion, and rocks rained down on the barn. At the same time, we heard what sounded like a car hitting our barn, and we ran out to see what had happened. Sitting half in the side of a lean-to attached to the barn was the stump. It had flown about 25 feet and hit the shed and broke through the outer wall, pushing the wallboards and two 2 X 4s inside the barn. Ed looked at the damage for about five minutes and said, "Holy crap. Dad will be a little upset over this."

We re-harnessed the horses, tied onto the burl with the chain, and pulled it into the yard. After trimming the roots off, we worked on the barn to patch the hole. We fixed it good as new, but the paint was a bunch redder than the existing paint, and it looked like a red Band-Aid on the outside wall.

When Dad came home, he never mentioned or asked what went on while he was gone to St. Paul except to tell Ed, that if we were going to paint the barn, that was one funny place to start.

1941

Herb Ott, Cattle Buyer

I was born in 1928 on a farm in Floyd County, Iowa, right in the horrible time of the Great Depression. Being a farm kid, I very seldom went into town, so I missed the fun and games that city kids took for granted. When I was allowed to go into town, Mother said that I needed exposure to the distinct difference between city and rural environments. Since my dad was a train engineer, he spent a whole lot of time away from our farm, and in the process, he laid claim to a whole herd of friends, some good and a few that were moochers. A good handful of the whole bunch was interested in getting Dad to start a still to use up some of our good field corn. They were the ones who had a terrific and ongoing thirst for any liquid that contained alcohol, liniment, and even a small kick of paint thinner. But Dad never had a still—even though the sheriff figured that he did. Every winter we had an influx of "acquaintances" who visited for hours.

There were a few I talked to and liked, but there also were a few that I really did not feel comfortable with. I figured that, if they thought we were doing anything illegal, they'd bust their garters reporting it to the sheriff. A few of the so-called friends had been busted by the law themselves, but usually only served a few days in the Crow Bar Hotel before they were bonded out by some unknown benefactor—everyone knew it was the sheriff—and were ordered to ferret out illegal goings-on in the county.

In those days, lawsuits were a novelty...

One of those employed stool birds happened to tell my brother Ed that he'd split the sheriff's reward of $100 with him if Ed would give him a tip on anything illegal taking place in the area. He just happened to be intoxicated sitting in the pool hall when Ed walked in. Evidently, he didn't connect Ed with the Anderson clan. Ed told me that he got even with one of our sour-assed neighbors by telling the drunk that he had smelled the odor of cooking mash every time he went by the neighbor's farm. Ed also knew that the farmer's silo leaked silage juice all over the barnyard, and occasionally the owner would load up a manure spreader with a bunch of that stinky and gooey mess and dump it by his fence line. That had created an on-going odor that closely resembled discarded mash. The drunk ran to tattle to the sheriff, and when he found out that the tip came from one of the Andersons, a deputy attempted to scare the truth out of the farmer. When the truth finally came out, the farmer's oldest son, a tough man of 18, caught the deputy behind the theatre and beat the dog-crap out of him. In those days, lawsuits were a novelty, and the farmer's son went unscathed. The deputy enforced the law with a pair of black eyes and a caverness hole where his left front tooth had been at anchor for 30 some years. After that, the only time a farmer was busted was when he was actually caught selling alcohol or the law found a live still.

Dad's friends were a mixed bag...

During those visits with Dad's friends, I added a whole bunch of words to my vocabulary that I didn't dare use. Quite a few were beyond my knowledge, and I never used them, but when these old men caught me listening to their so-called conversation, I was warned never to repeat anything or I'd have my tongue bobbed. I knew that meant they'd split my tongue, so I promised to never divulge a single word. One of Dad's friends was a cattle buyer for the auction yards. The yards held auctions for anything and everything they could get hold of, from farm animals to dogs and cats and even a chimpanzee that was supposedly tame. The chimp, however, didn't stick with his buyer because he tried to pull the buyer's wife's hair out by the roots.

In those days, everyone had pets instead of money. The pets consisted of cats, rabbits, dogs, skunks, squirrels, opossums, pigeons, doves, and maybe even a red fox. We claimed a big yellow cat, a collie dog, a ground hog, one goat, a weasel, and one garter snake. I even kept a small turtle in a fish bowl and a frog that kept it company. We also furnished a home for a pair of skunks, but they weren't pets. My brother claimed that the snake kept mice away from the barn. Our pets all had their quirks. Our dog would help a thief if he petted her, and the ground hog would just jump down the nearest hole, grunting like a pig. We also kept a big grey and white female goose, but she wasn't a pet except to my mother. The goose attacked everyone but Mom, hissing and flapping her big wings, which hurt like hell when she hit you with them. It seemed like the goose hated me most of all, so I walked a wide birth around her. There was also a big hoot owl that sat on our back fence at night, but all he did was holler "Who, who."

Dad's cattle buyer friend was Herb Ott, but everyone called him "Shorts." He came by several times a year to ask us to consign something for auction. He told us he would take anything to auction. He especially wanted calves, pigs, and Mom's old grey goose. He told Mother that the goose was a prize and that he would give her $50 for her on the spot, but the goose and Mother were partners in the egg noodle business, and Mom wouldn't sell.

Besides, the goose liked Mom and let Mom pet and hand feed her, but no one else.

Herb just disappeared from sight...

Herb seemed to be a straightforward person, and unlike some of Dad's so-called friends, he was not overly friendly. Herb was a short, round man, all of 5′ 6″ tall, and his bowler hat sat on the top of his head like an oatmeal bowl. The hat had a two-inch brim and pushed his ears forward so it looked like he was an eager listener. Herb was as bald as a pealed onion, but the hat hid that fact, as he had a good crop of grey hair on the back of his head and around his ears. The suit he wore was a little small, and he walked with his shoulders back like he was strutting, and that pushed his stomach out in front. But, outside of that Derby hat, the too-small clothes, and a stomach that poked out of his jacket and preceded him by about eight inches, he was okay. My brother Ed related Herb to Charlie Chaplin because he resembled him some. I didn't like to get too close to him when he was talking because he had a real bad case of bad breath.

One Sunday in 1939, Herb drove into the yard on one of his regular visits and parked by a small but deep ditch I had dug to water some bushes. When it was hot and dry, I would pump water into the ditch, and it carried water to raspberry bushes behind the house. Herb didn't know the ditch was there, as it was overgrown with grass. When Herb shut the car down, he just sat there with his arm on the door, and I wondered if he was going to get out. After about five minutes, he opened the door and stepped out, unaware of the deep little ditch. I was watching him, and when he slid out of the car, he just seemed to disappear from sight. I waited for him to come around the back of the car, but he didn't, and I wondered where he went. I walked around the car, and there Herb lay, flat on his back with one foot in the ditch and his funny hat about six feet away on the opposite side of the ditch. I had pumped water the day before, and mud from the ditch covered Herb's jacket. I heard Herb groan, and I figured that he had the wind knocked out of him, but no broken bones. He looked up, saw me standing there, stuck out his hand, and said, "Don't just stand there, Kid. Help me to my feet."

I walked over, grabbed his hand, and pulled as hard as I could. It was like trying to lift a gunnysack full of corn or oats. I was trying to lift a 250-pound giant, and I only weighed about 80 pounds. All the time I was pulling on him, he was grunting like a hog in an apple orchard. He sounded like he was helping, but I could tell he wasn't using any effort to get up. I couldn't budge him, and as my hand slipped off his, I fell backwards. That surprised him, and he uttered, "Oh, sh**," as I climbed to my feet.

Our big, grey goose was watching us, and I knew Herb was afraid of being attacked. I asked Herb if he could roll over onto his stomach, and he nodded. But after three tries, I had to roll him over like a barrel. I grabbed his hand, and with Herb helping some, we got him to his feet. The second he was erect, Mother's goose rushed at him, flapping her wings and hissing like a snake. It scared him real bad. I had to yell and wave my arms to stop the goose. Herb staggered over to his car and leaned on the fender. He was panting like a race runner, and it took a few minutes for him to get his breath. Then he said, "By God, Kid. I just knew I was dying, a goner for sure. I could hear organ music and someone talking like from the sky."

I looked at him, and he was sweating pretty good, so I told him that what he heard was one of Mother's soap operas she listened to every day. I mentioned that she had the kitchen window open, and that was what he heard.

Old Billy helped out where he could...

Herb finally calmed down and asked if my dad was around. When I told him no, he said, "Oh, sh**," once more and then tried to wipe the mud off his coat. All he did was smear it real good, and then he walked around the car and headed for our water tank. I just hoped he wouldn't fall into the tank because I knew I wouldn't be able to pull him out and he'd, sure as the sky was blue, just drown. He bent over the water tank, splashing water on his coat, and I turned around to see where our goat was. Billy was a black and white goat, had long, curved horns, and weighed about 100 pounds before breakfast. He was also real fast on his legs and could outrun me when he headed for the barn. The crazy goat hated everyone but me, and he had free run of the yard and watched everything.

One week before, he had an encounter with a salesman and flattened him out real good, so when he saw this fat little man bent over the tank, he just reacted naturally. He was about 50 feet away, and I saw him start towards Herb, so I hollered for Herb to watch out, but by the time Herb straightened up, the goat planted his two horns right on the back of Herb's lap. That goat was doing about 25 miles an hour, and Herb became airborne. He lit up against the water tank, making noise like a sack of grain thrown into our hayrack. He rolled back from the tank and ended up on his back. I heard him yell out, "Oh sh**," again, and then he yelled, "Oh man, I think I'm broken all to pieces."

When Herb had fallen after the goat butted him, his pants had split open, and he looked like one of the hobos I used to see from time to time. His jacket was all muddy, and he had lost his hat, his glasses, and most of his dignity. When I helped him up, he called our goat quite a few adjectives, but I had heard most of them before. I had forgotten to tell Herb that our goat was a hazard on our place and to beware when he got out of his car, but I guess he knew now. I finally got Herb up again, and he said, "All I want to do is get the dickens out of here." He walked unsteadily to his car, crawled in, and just sat there for a minute or two. Then he started the car and drove away. I sat on the porch thinking what a pitiful sight that poor man had become in such a short time. Our dog Sandy had licked Herb on the face, and I figured that even the dog felt bad.

Just a few minutes had gone by when Herb drove back into the yard. He yelled at me, "Hey, Kid, I want my glasses and wallet back." I walked over to his car and asked him where he had left them. Herb climbed out of the car, shoved his hat back on his head, and said, "What do you mean, 'Where in the hell did I leave them?' Holy horse sh**, Kid, I thought you picked them up where I fell." I told him I had never seen his glasses or his wallet. I walked over to where Herb had fallen into the ditch, and there in the ditch were his glasses and his wallet. I gathered them up, went over to Herb's car, and threw them onto the passenger seat. As he drove away, Mother said, "Good riddance." I quietly agreed, but never said a word.

My buddy Fats said that Shorty had come to their farm too, looking to get some consigned stock, and that Fats' dog, Carson, bit him on the leg. Fats said that Herb had told his mother that no one seemed to like him, not even dogs. Fats told me that he didn't care for Herb because he saw Herb try to get Carson into his car in an attempt to steal him.

He was fat enough to qualify...

Later that fall, Herb just seemed to disappear, and I never saw him again. A few weeks later, word went around about an accident on a distant farm. The story was that Herb had called on an elderly farmer north of the school and was a little careless. He had stepped onto the hay net full of hay, and the hired man had pulled the net up to the haymow before he saw Herb dangling by one leg about 15 feet in the air. Herb was lucky the lift tractor shut down before he ended up in the haymow or he could have really been hurt bad. After the hired man extricated Herb, he gave Herb a darn good cussin' out and threatened to beat the crap out of him if he ever came back again.

Dad told me that Herb was totally upset and had cussed out the farmer, his hired man, and his son and said they had tried to kill him. Then he sat in his Model A and cried, sobbing pretty loud. The farmer gave Herb a $20 bill, got him a little pain killer in a pint jar, and sent him on his way.

Fats told me that lifting up a hog by the leg was how they butchered all porkers, and that Herb was real lucky that he had human clothes on, because he was fat enough to qualify.

1940

Homer Pressler

In June of 1939, the first month of summer vacation from the dreaded sixth grade, I was happier than a robin in a garden patch pulling worms. For the next three months, there would be no school, and outside of a few chores, I could do the more important things in life, like chasing frogs, turtles, and hornet nests. I could also keep track of what was news in our neck-of-the-woods. I was almost an adult—I would be 11 years old on August 28—and in a few years, I would be able to vote. I planned to vote against everyone then in office and to give some other poor people a chance to get rich like the senators did. Dad always said that, if you could get elected to federal office, you'd be rich in a year or two. Then you could get fat, wear good clothes, lie and steal, and never be jailed. And then, you could run for re-election and do it all over again.

Hitler was taking over countries like a coyote after rabbits...

Our Atwater-Kent radio kept us informed about many of the war developments. Europe was somewhat settled down for the moment, and everyone hoped Hitler was done killing. I figured that he would take over Africa and India next. Then he would gobble up Russia like a chicken gobbling up a June bug. Everyone said I was nuts because Russia was too big for little Germany to whip, but Hitler was taking over countries like a coyote goes after rabbits and adding them to his 1,000-year Reich. He had Mussolini, another lunatic in Italy, who had the same goals, and the two of them wanted to share the world.

There was a German farmer, who lived about three miles east of our farm and who did not like Germany one bit. I visited with him once in a while, but it was a chore because he drank quite a bit, chewed tobacco, and loved garlic. He was Dad's old friend, and his name was Homer Pressler. Sometimes, he would come to visit, and he'd bring his wife with him. He called her Myrna Lily, and she was a large lady, who sometimes cussed.

Myrna and my mother would sit in the living room darning, fixing clothing, and drinking green tea. All farm kids were really tough on clothes, and every month or so, Myrna helped Mother repair our well-used clothes. By the time they had repaired all the clothes, they had also thoroughly discussed happenings in several big towns in Germany, including Dresden. Then they would cook up a big supper, and we would eat everything on the table. Then, still visiting,

Dad and Mom would slowly walk Homer and Myrna out to their old Ford coupe. Homer would follow along behind, and when he got to the car, he would offer all of us a smart slug of corn from a pint fruit jar kept in the rumble seat on the Model A. Dad told me that sometimes it was good to take a sip socially—especially because Homer cooked up his own medical juice. Sometimes Dad would take some, but most times, he would decline. Then we would visit up 'til the time Homer started the Model A and began backing up to leave, and we would wave until the car was out of sight.

Homer was a quiet sort of person and never did talk too much. He always said, "Hello, young fellow," and would reach out and shake my hand. He was skinny, smoked a corncob pipe that had one side almost burned away, and chewed string tobacco. Between sucking on the pipe and spitting every few minutes, he didn't have time to talk too much. Dad did most of the talking, with Homer spitting every few moments, nodding his head, "Yes," and saying, "Yup," to everything Dad said. I figured that Homer thought that Dad knew everything about everything.

Once in a while, I'd hear Dad say to Homer, "How's my friend Homer, the Dumb-o-crat?" And Homer would say, "As good as any retread Re-publican-eer." Homer was a real hard Democrat and had voted for Roosevelt twice. He always wore a pin on his shirt that said "Vote." He wore cotton long underwear year 'round and rolled his shirt sleeves up to his elbows. Generally, the sleeves of his underwear would be ragged and soiled.

Homer was 70 years old, and he really liked a nip of corn...

One day that summer, Homer and Myrna came to visit. When he drove through our gate, he scraped the side of the gate. He had never done that before, and I thought he was drinking. He drove the car up to the front porch and shut it off. Homer slid out of the car and walked around the car to help Myrna. She was mad and pushed Homer away. I ran down to the barn to tell Dad that Homer was here. When Dad got up to the house, Homer was sitting on the porch, smoking his pipe. He said, "Art, come here and sit a spell." I sat on the fender of Homer's car and took in most of their conversation. I heard Homer tell Dad that, a few days back, he had been pinched for careless driving. He said that the cop that had arrested him had also accused him of drinking but had agreed to let Homer go if he would say where he acquired the corn or who sold it to him.

When he didn't squeal on anyone or tell where the alcohol came from, the dirty s.o.b. just escorted him down to the Crowbar Hotel and pushed him into a dirty, stinking cell. The stained cot stunk like a skunk with bad breath, and there was no way to get water. The only part of the incarceration that wasn't too bad was the fact that there were no rats—evidently it was too filthy for their taste.

Homer said that he was in that box for three days, and then the Justice of the Peace let his wife Myrna put up the ten dollars' bond and ordered him to appear in court in two weeks to discuss the charges. Homer asked Dad what he could do to soften the mess he was in. Dad sat there for what seemed like an hour before he answered Homer. First off, he said, "Dammit, Homer. You're almost 70 years old. Why in the devil did you drink and then drive your car into town? You should have stayed home. If you tell the judge the truth, you'll get a big fine and do six months in the county jail, and that cop will be a hero. The county will make headlines for busting a still ran by the biggest hog raiser in the county."

Homer sat there, quiet as a mouse with a bellyache, looking at the ground. Then he wiped his shirt across his eyes, spit, and said, "Art, I feel terrible. I should have stayed home or just not have taken a drink. What can I do to extricate myself from all of this mess? If I don't get out of it, Myrna will nag me for the rest of my life."

Shades of grey...

Dad just sat there for a few minutes without speaking; then he looked at Homer and said, "I think we can get you off with just a fine. When you appear before the judge, don't say anything to anyone until the judge calls you to the stand. Don't say even one word. When the judge asks you what you have to say about the arrest, speak right up and tell your story. Think on what I said now, and go to your car and fetch back what's left of your pint of moonshine. Set the jar on the ground beside the steps after you wipe it down good. And leave it there when you head for home. After you tell the judge you were guilty of speeding because you had to pick up your wife, tell him that you were also gawking around and weren't watching how fast you were going. Tell him how sorry you are that you broke the law and, for sure, you will never do it again. As for the drinking complaint, tell him that you and your wife had stopped to see the Andersons, and while you were sitting on the porch, you saw a jar by the steps. Tell him you opened the jar because it looked like kerosene and could have caused your friends a problem, so you took a sip, spit it out, and told your wife it was corn whiskey that someone had hid there. Tell the judge that you couldn't believe that there was any corn on the Anderson's farm, because the Andersons are law abiding, and it just couldn't be theirs. Then tell the judge that he can have the sheriff go out there now—the jar should still be there. Then don't say anymore."

Homer asked Dad what he would say if the cop did come by, and Dad said he'd tell the cop that the jar had been there for a couple of weeks and he that figured it belonged to one of Ed's friends. That way, Homer wouldn't have to lie to the judge any more than necessary.

Homer asked Dad if he thought the judge would believe that story, and Dad said, "You bet—if you don't offer any other comments. I know him, and he sure as heck won't call both of us liars. When you leave the courthouse, stop by and fill me in, and be sure and take $100 in change so you can pay the fine with the exact amount. Remember, Homer, the J.P. will get part of the fine for a misdemeanor, but if you go to jail, he won't get a cent..."

When Homer came by that next Monday, he drove into the yard and told me to tell Dad everything was okay. That Friday night, he drove into the yard, climbed out of his car, and walked over to the barn where we were feeding the cows. He grabbed Dad's hand and almost shook it loose from his shoulder. He said, "By damn, Art, you're a genius. I did what you said, and when I told them to contact you, he said that wouldn't be necessary. He fined me $40 with a stern warning to obey all the laws from now on. I could have put a big kiss on his cheek."

When Homer left, Dad told me that sometimes a little grey tale wouldn't hurt. I figured that Dad was right and that Homer would be the better for Dad's help. Soon the word went around that our farm had a supply of excellent corn for sale. We had to chase away a few cars that came to buy booze. One of them offered my big brother $50 for one pint. Ed chased him away and told me that, if he had sold him any, the dummy would have drunk part of it and then turned us in for the reward.

After it was all over, Myrna told Mom that, if she ever left Homer, he'd end up in the old folks' home because Homer was so dumb he couldn't zip up his trousers without her help.

And then Homer told Dad that nobody knew it, but Myrna would take a few nips of his corn most nights, too. And so it went.

1941

Levi Welton, Farmer and Friend

I grew up on a farm in Floyd County, Iowa, in the hard times of the 1930s when times were harder than a piece of month-old home-baked white bread. No matter how you cut it, it was the worst time to grow up; at least that was what my big brother Ed used to say. The luxuries of life just didn't apply to farmers. There were no "eight-hour days," so there wasn't much time to relax and enjoy the so-called "easy" life of the farmer. During my early years, I was able to meet and learn the names of over 30 families. Most of the farmers were family men, blessed with children, and it seemed that most of those children were girls. I was extremely fortunate in that I had an older brother named Ed, who declared to me that he knew everything about everything. And he reminded me of that every so often so I wouldn't forget how blessed I was. There were only two farmers in the area that I knew who had never married. One of them lived on the border area with Minnesota and was a friend of my dad; the other loner lived only two miles from our farm, and his name was Levi Welton.

Old Levi was a lot older than I had thought…

One day, Dad told us that his old friend Levi Welton was coming down from Waverly to talk to him about something personal. Dad said that he would be driving an old black buggy behind an old grey horse and that we were to make him welcome. Dad said he would be out cutting some wild hay and to tell his friend to have a cup of coffee and to relax until Dad finished cutting the hay. Dad hitched our team of horses to the mower and headed out to cut the hay before his friend arrived. I sat down by the big oak tree and tried to finish a book about the sinking of the Titanic. That book scared the liver out of me, and I vowed never to take a trip on a big boat.

I was just about done reading the book when this older man pulled into the yard, driving a buggy pulled by an ancient grey horse. The horse just plodded along, putting one foot in front of the other, and stopped by where I was sitting. He snorted, shook his head, and just seemed to fall asleep. The driver was a giant of a man, and he filled up the whole seat of the buggy, which leaned to the left. He slapped the reins down on the grey, and the horse moved up to the water tank and stopped. I had seen the driver a few times, and it had to be Levi Welton. He slid down off the buggy seat and leaned against the wheel, where he had one doozy of a coughing fit. It lasted about three minutes, and I watched him try to get his breath. He ended up leaning over the buggy wheel, gasping and holding a ragged old, red neckerchief over his mouth. He stood there for quite a while, and I could see he was older than I thought. He had on a pair of old cotton plaid pants and an old pair of long johns that needed to be junked.

He finally walked over to the back porch and sat on the edge, looking at me. His left shoe had a good-sized hole in the toe part, and it didn't appear to me that he had any socks on, but that was normal, as lots of people didn't wear socks or underwear if they wore long johns. It seemed that most of the older farmers used safety pins to hold their clothes together. This was especially true of the front part of their overalls called the barn door. Levi sat still for a few moments and then he pulled out an old corncob pipe. It sounded like he had the heaves as he lit about a dozen matches trying to get it lit. He sucked on the horrible smelling thing for a moment or two and then asked, "Is your Pa anywhere around so I can talk to him?" I told him my dad was out cutting hay and would be back in a few minutes. Levi said, "Yep, sure as the devil likes heat, it'll be one hell of a cold winter. You fellas are gonna need more hay this year."

Don't dig the hole yet, Levi, you just need to find a little filly...

Levi stood up, took a step towards his buggy, and had another coughing fit for a few minutes. He coughed so hard that he bent over and put his hands on his knees. His pipe fell out of his hand, and I figured that his pipe was causing his problem. This friend of Dad's was older than I thought, and I felt sorry for him. I also felt sorry for the old horse, which appeared to be on his last legs. Dad had told me that old Levi had never been hitched, and they became friends when they played softball together for the Charles City team. Dad was a train engineer, and Levi was a shift foreman at the Hart-Parr Tractor Company. Levi had an 80-acre farm, and I had been up to it a few times. He had a passel of chickens and a pair of brown mules that had the run of the farm. He did sip a little corn and carried a vinegar jar full of it in the buggy, but he was a slow, kind old man, and I liked him.

Dad came up to the barn a little later, unhitched the horses, and came walking over to the porch. Levi and Dad talked for about five minutes; then Dad went into the house and came back with his car keys. He told me to jump into the back seat of the car while he climbed into the front with Levi. We drove out of the yard and headed for town. On the way, Levi had a couple of spells, and I figured we were taking him to the doctor. I heard him tell Dad that he had a bad case of the heaves, and he said he probably wouldn't make it to Christmas. That scared me, and I said a silent prayer for the old man. Dad said, "Don't dig the hole yet, Levi. We'll wait and see what the doctor says." When we got to the doctor's place, I had to wait in the car. Dad went with Levi, and they were gone a long time.

When they came out to the car, Dad was grinning, and Levi was wasting matches trying to light up his pipe. They climbed into the car, and Dad said that Levi was in pretty good shape, but he had, over the years, breathed in too much dust from hay and dirt. He said Levi would be better off to stay out of the barn and hire a man to help him. He also said that Levi should put an exhaust fan in the barn to keep the dust down. I had never seen my dad show any emotion except when an animal died or when someone he was friends with passed away. All the way home, Levi kept telling Dad what a good, generous friend he was and kept thanking Dad all the way home for his care. I could tell that he was so happy that the doctor had given him some hope for a cure, that he heaped praise on Dad in relief.

When we arrived home, Dad visited with Levi about his old, burned-out pipe and told him that he should quit smoking, throw away the pipe, find a little filly, and get married up. Dad said, "Levi, let's face it. You need someone to share your life with. Spend some time in town, find a lady friend, and buy a new car. Put the old buggy in the shed, turn the old grey out to pasture, and sell off your livestock. Do some traveling and use up some of the money you got buried in those coffee cans." Levi looked at Dad and handed him the pipe.

He was found with an old three-tined hayfork in his hand …

Levi walked out to his old buggy, grunted a few times, and climbed into it. He picked up the reins, slapped them gently against the old grey's back, and drove out of the yard, lifting his right hand up as a parting gesture. Dad threw the pipe into a garbage can by the porch and said, "Albert, old Levi will be back; he's pretty sick, and the doctor was just being kind. If Levi sees Christmas come and go, I'll be real surprised. His lungs are in real bad shape. He has something called 'consumption,' and it's usually fatal. Don't you ever use tobacco—it is poison." Then he told me that one of these days Levi would start to cough and would be unable to stop. Dad thought a few minutes and then said, "I'll sure miss that old codger when he goes. He's one honest man, who never asked for anything and never said a bad word about anybody."

On the December 23, 1938, Dad came home from St. Paul, Minnesota, and told us that old Levi had died in his barn feeding his few cows hay. He fell in front of the stanchions and was found with an old three-tined hayfork in his right hand. The funeral was sparsely attended, and Levi's only family, a lady about 90 years old, bid Levi good-bye. I had never seen her before, and that was the first time I saw my dad cry.

1941

Little Brown Church

Many, many Sundays, I listened to my mother sing softly about a little brown church in the vale as I was getting myself ready to go to church and Sunday school in Charles City, Iowa. My mother had a habit of singing and humming a few religious hymns while she was fixing breakfast in the kitchen, and I sometimes hummed them while I was doing chores. Of all the hymns I listened to, there were two that were my favorites. *The Old Rugged Cross* was number one

all of my life, but the one that rattled around in my head and that I memorized every word of was *The Little Brown Church in the Vale.* That was a song about an active, non-denominational church in Nashua, Iowa, just down the highway about five miles.

Our farm was in Floyd County, almost exactly in the middle between Charles City and the town of Nashua.

As far back as I can remember, the little church was talked and sung about and was the most revered place of worship in

Little Brown Church. Nashua, Iowa.

northeastern Iowa. People came from miles

70

around to attend and worship in the church. They left with a grand and elated feeling that the church was a wonderful place to worship. It was truly a special place. Over the years between the 1920s and the year that we moved away, 1943, hundreds of passers-by, tourists, and a good cross section of various religious affiliated people sat in the small church and were welcomed by everyone. There were also weddings, funerals, and special occasions that filled the pews from time to time. Almost everyone who left after the service felt better off.

The popularity of the church was so great and its song so well dispersed throughout the country that, after the war ended in 1946, attendance rapidly increased, and the church was renovated to accommodate the greater number of parishioners. I recall one Sunday while attending the little church that the Minister gave a sermon on the Ten Commandments and their real meaning. He said that those rules were not just words, but were a set of rules containing a multitude of inferences to many guidelines that all Christians must follow to remain Christians and should not knowingly break. After that session, I attended the little church many times and always looked forward to attending so I could be a part of that congregation. I also came to realize that human frailties were a major factor in life, but I knew of no one who had ever committed a violation of the Ten Commandments. Sundays at the little church helped a whole bunch of people conduct their daily lives in a more Christian manner.

Never ever discuss religion in school…

Early in 1943, we moved north of Charles City into a different school district, so we had a new school, known as the Line School, and we had to break in a new teacher, Miss Heise. We soon figured out that this teacher was more forceful, was stricter, and tolerated less monkey- and prank-business than our old teacher, Miss Crouse. One day during study time, I was telling a classmate about the great Little Brown Church. The teacher told me to come to the front of the room and tell everyone what was more interesting than tomorrow's lessons. When I ended telling the whole class about the church in the vale, she sternly reminded me that one must never ever discuss religion in her school, but a lot of the kids were interested, and during recess, we ended up in a bunch while I answered their questions concerning the Little Brown Church. I wasn't the most learned person concerning the church, but I did tell them everything I knew. Then, during class, I wrote out the words to *The Little Brown Church in the Vale* and let some of them copy the song. The next week, quite a few of the kids were humming the song during recess. Needless to say, I was severely reprimanded and told to stop discussing the church. But what upset her most was that the church was not in our district; at least, that is what I thought.

That Friday, I stayed in the school during recess and asked Miss Heise why we weren't allowed to talk about the little brown church in school. She looked at me for a bit and then said, "For your information, our Constitution forbids any effort to sponsor, promote, or favor any one religion as the only one to attend. A few of our founding fathers came from Europe and left behind the prosecution imposed on non-Catholics, so when the framers of the Constitution met to commit it to writing, they made sure that the signers were not allowed to support any one religion." Miss Heise looked at me very intently and said, "I have a copy of the Constitution and the Bill of Rights that you can take home and study—you can bring it back on Monday."

Sometimes kids get it right and adults don't...

I did as she suggested and took it home; I read both documents a few times and then returned them. My only comment to Miss Heise was, "The Little Brown Church always welcomes everyone, and it is non-denominational. I've been there for Sunday services, and I'm a Lutheran. Our neighbor is a Catholic, and he is there every Sunday. My other neighbor is a Methodist, and he comes all the time."

I looked at her, and all she said was, "Why don't you go out and play with the rest of the class."

1947

Blackie

When I was 12 and growing up on our farm, we had an accumulation of stock. We had pigs, chickens, milk cows, Herefords, and horses—both Belgian workhorses and riding stock. We also supported quite a few prairie dogs, chicken hawks, pheasants, rabbits, and snakes, even though we never owned these freeloaders. We did own one old Hereford bull that was extremely docile and retired, ready for the meat cutter.

One of my dad's self-appointed yearly chores was to bring a humongous Hereford bull from our neighbor to mingle with our cows. Hereford cattle were predominantly raised in our area, and it was deemed necessary to keep the genetics strong.

Blackie was the name of the bull Dad brought home. They called him Blackie because he had a black spot on his left hip about the size of a dinner plate. Most bulls are big, but it seemed that Blackie was bigger than most. I mean he was biggg. He stood about five feet tall, and his owner listed him as weighing 2,000+ pounds. Now, that was dry weight, right out of the barn with no breakfast. He had horns cut off at the ends and hooves as big as a Clydesdale horse. I swear to this day that I could have walked under that bull and never tickled his stomach. He was about eight years old, and when he arched his neck and bellered, you could hear him for a mile. He had slobbers on the sides of his mouth, and he scared me pretty bad.

My brother had to put Blackie in a holding pen for a few days to relax. The pen was a 25-foot square enclosure, double fenced with two rows of wire. My dad always called those few days "S & D" time so the bull could build up his stamina and determination for later.

After about three days, he had a tankful of "S & D"...

I spent several hours by that double fence, just watching that bull watching me. He drooled like he was hungry, and I would make a good meal. My brother Ed told me that the bull had eaten a black dog and that was why they called him Blackie. Finally after about three days, Blackie had a full tank of "S & D" and began to pace.

Hereford bull with a nose ring and an attitude.

I was watching him one morning when he spotted the small herd of cows at our windmill and water tank in the adjacent field. He perked up, and his ears shot out forward as he lumbered towards the fence. He slid to a halt and raised his head and bellered. What an awful sound came out of his mouth. The cows all quit drinking and turned to look at the bull. After a few moments, they started for the enclosure at a walk and then quickly increased their speed. As I watched them come towards us, it looked like a small stampede. I thought the cows would mow down the fences to get to Ed. He just laughed! He knew something I didn't; in addition to the "S & D" time, the bull also had restored his "D & A" time — desire and anticipation.

Ed confided in me that he knew everything, even bulls...

While the cows milled at the fence, that bull carried on something fierce. He began bellowing, swinging his tail, pawing at the ground, and butting at the fence. I knew that he had gone nuts for no apparent reason. My mother didn't appear to be concerned, however, so I knew it must be all right. Besides, the holding fence was five feet tall and made of hog wire. The security fence was about one foot away from it and was made of six-strand barbwire. There was about 12" of post protruding over the top of both fences. About the only thing that could get through it was a Milwaukee S-2 engine.

My brother Ed was long and thin, 16 years old, and the self-proclaimed head of our farm. My father was an engineer for the railroad and gone quite a bit, so he always left Ed in charge. Ed confided in me that he knew everything. He also said he knew all about bulls and could handle any old bull with nothing but a pitchfork. He gave some rules to follow around bulls: don't get too close to any bull, don't tease them with a stick, keep the water tank full, and don't feed them. I obeyed, but I thought Ed misread the bull's age, and I didn't think Blackie was afraid of anything, especially a pitchfork.

Ed wasn't scared, he was just cautious, or so he said...

The day we turned Blackie out into the pasture is unforgettable. Ed had a three-tined pitchfork that he was going to use to prod the bull out the gate to the pasture. Ed opened the double gate and entered the pen. Blackie was standing in the far corner, and when he saw Ed, he let out a horrible roar. He pawed the ground, throwing dirt over each shoulder, grunting, and frothing at the mouth. Looking back, I can still see Ed holding that small three-tined pitchfork out towards that bull. I'm sure that Ed was hoping that the bull would just exit the pen and prove him right again. Now Ed wasn't the bravest warrior I knew, not like Tarzan or Hoot Gibson. I also knew that knowing and doing just weren't related when it came to giant bulls that were madder than a stepped-on snake, but I had to watch.

The closer Ed came to that bull, the madder Blackie became. All at once, he lowered his head, pointed his tail at the sky, and charged. The sound he made as he charged would have scared any normal person. Ed later told me that he just wasn't scared, only cautious. It took Ed about five seconds to get his feet to work, and he started toward the fence with the pitchfork. I asked him later why he didn't throw the pitchfork away, and he replied, "What fork?" If the bull hadn't slipped, he would have won the race for sure. Ed was running like a turpentined-cat, yelling, "Close the gate!" He never made the fence on the first try, and the bull ran right over him, ripping his shirt and making a few bloody spots on his back. That massive hunk of hamburger slid around for another try, and Ed scrambled for the fence where I stood. Ed grabbed the top of the fence post and cleared both fences in one mighty leap.

Hamburger wasn't worth a dollar a pound...

I stood there at the fence and heard Ed yell to my mother to bring him the shotgun. That gun was a 12 gauge double barrel loaded with No. 9 buckshot for prowlers, revenuers, coyotes, and foxes that became too friendly. (I still have the shotgun.) Mother brought the gun to Ed, and he was aiming it at the bull when my dad drove into the yard. He slid to a stop and yelled at Ed to put the gun down. Ed stood there like one of those Chinese warriors: shirt tore almost off, bloody, and plumb white. I listened while Dad lectured my brother and reprimanded him for being so careless that he might have damaged that bull. I never said a word.

My dad told Ed that, if he shot the bull in the head, it probably wouldn't have killed him, but it probably would have made him mad enough to charge the fence. He also told Ed that, if he had tried just to scare the bull, the buckshot might have caught him in the rear end and caused a major change in the bull's anatomy, ability, and attitude. Either way, we would have had to buy the bull and doctor him, or eat him and pay for the privilege. And hamburger wasn't worth a dollar a pound.

That fall, Dad bought a new bull for the genetic upkeep of our herd and bought a new Buick. He gave Ed the Model A Ford and sent him to town to school, and Blackie never came back to visit the girls. Amen.

1946

Carson

During the spring of 1943, when Fats and I had graduated from the eighth grade, Fats' sister hit marrying age and planned a June wedding ceremony to be held on their farm. Her boyfriend was in the Navy, and he was due for a furlough—he would be home June 15 for two weeks. Everyone in a large radius of their farm was invited, including all of the junior and senior kids. It would be a big party of eating, dancing, and just a whole lot of visiting. There would be all kinds of pies, cakes, ice cream, and a real humdinger of a dinner. All the farm wives were constantly meeting, planning what and how much to provide. Even the dogs seemed to know something was going on because our shepherd Sandy barked every time the ladies came to our house. I believe he could smell the odor of good cooking on their clothes.

We figured Jimmy would come to his senses eventually…

There were seven farms getting ready for the wedding, stockpiling gifts and appliances to start the new farmers off right. Fats and I both got new shoes and jackets to wear, and the girls bought new dresses or made their own to match the pink and white colors of the bride. The two weeks to the nuptials went by slowly and without mishap. We could hardly wait to attend the grand ceremony and all the coming festivities. We all knew Jimmy, the groom, and everyone thought he was great.

There was only one problem that my friends and I could put our finger on—why was he giving up all the good times we usually had swimming, fishing, and hunting pheasants—just for a girl? Even Fats thought Jim was addled or had been shell-shocked or mentally injured during the war. Fats said that, when Jim came to the house to see Julie, his sister, he didn't act right. He didn't joke or wrestle with the dog, Carson. He said, "please" and "thank you" to the folks, and that had to be a sure sign of losing your mind. Jimmy only wanted to sit in the house with Julie instead of hunting frogs and turtles in the creek. Also, he wore clean clothes, and his boots were shined all the time.

Fats had a crush on one of the Miller girls once, but that sure didn't change the way he always was. Holy mackerel, anyone who turned down a second or even a third piece of apple pie had to be going loony. We all figured that Jim would come to his senses at the last minute and run, so we decided we would all treat him good and hope for the best. If he showed up for the nuptials, we figured to dunk him in the water tank.

Happiness—or was that sympathy—for Jimmy…

The fatal day came on bright, clear, and dry… a perfect day for the humongous ceremony about to take place. The big red barn would see the grand event of its life. The wedding was to take place at 2:00 p.m., and no one knew when it would end. My family piled into our car, and Dad drove the five miles to the scene. When we arrived, it somewhat resembled a county fair. Cars and buggies were parked everywhere. We entered the barn and found about 50 people sitting on rows of chairs on the dance floor. The barn was decorated with ribbons and flowers, with candles on the reception table. An altar was erected at the front, with an altar table for the Bible surrounded with candles. A white wooden lattice surrounded the altar. As we sat down, I heard Fats' brother remark that he had made the whole thing all by himself.

The sermon went great, and I was in awe of what it took to get hitched. The happy couple finally tied the knot, and the preacher told Jim he could kiss the bride. It was a long embrace, and Fats remarked, "What's the big hairy deal anyway? That's all they do when he comes to the house, at least most of the time."

After a few minutes, the newlyweds came to the back of the barn floor to stand by the table where the punch bowl sat. Almost everyone attending walked by the table with congratulations and/or condolences while Fats and I drank punch. Quite a few of the ladies had dewy-eyes, and some of the men blew their noses a few times. Fats asked me if the dewy-eyes and runny noses were happy signs, or if they were caused from the home-brew his dad had put into the punch, or if they were signs of sympathy for Jimmy's predicament? I didn't know…

After everything quieted down, the dancing began, and it was the greatest dance I ever attended. Everyone danced with everyone, except Jim, who sat out most of the dances. The band was good and extra loud and played many different songs. Looking back, it played almost exactly like the Cushman Orchestra.

The dog days of summer…

They quit for supper after a couple of hours, and Fats and I went outside through the side door to churn the ice cream. Fats' dog Carson came out with us to help with the two churns, licking his chops all the while. We had a small dish that we used to sample the churned milk to make sure of its progress. We let Carson lick up the residue, and he loved it.

Earlier that spring, the county health nurse had put on a program titled, "The Deadly Threat of Rabies." Many of the local farmers attended with their kids. It was probably the scariest thing I had ever seen. It included pictures of rabid animals and listed skunks and dogs as the most likely suspects. The meeting included the term "dog days of August." Now everyone knew that "dog days" were coming in the summer and that July and August were the worst months. All dogs became meaner during the summer, and you could tell if a dog had rabies if it growled a lot, slunk around people, barked all the time, or frothed at the mouth.

When we had finished churning the ice cream, we put it into two large bowls: one bowl we left covered with a lid and sitting in a pan of ice, and the other bowl we set on the dessert table. Everyone was eating and having a fine time. Then Carson came walking onto the barn floor, and the first thing Fats and I heard was a loud shriek and then a bunch more yells. Some of the men were yelling, "Mad dog! Mad dog!"

There was uncontrolled panic among all the participants—tipping chairs and scrambling to get away from a mad dog. Poor

Carson just stood in the middle of the dance floor with white foam dripping from his mouth, eyes pointed forward. One man of about 300 pounds pushed past me and said, "Run for your life, Kid! Hydrophobia's deadly."

Another man shouted, "That dog's got rabies!"

Needless to say, the barn emptied rather quickly, including the bride and groom and the preacher. Quite a few cars left the area—fast. Fats and I stood watching Carson until he came over to the table, wagging his tail.

Fats went out to the ice cream makers and came right back. It seemed that Carson liked the ice cream so much he had somehow removed the lid of the bowl of ice cream sitting in the ice pan and ate almost all of the contents. There was no real cause for alarm, but he looked just like a rabid animal. The get-together unwound real quick. Everyone felt horrible later.

The next day, Fats' mother called all the participants and explained what had transpired. Fats later told me that they didn't have much company for a week or two, and those who came calling looked all around the house before getting out of their cars. Jim and his new bride left for California the next weekend, and I never saw them again. They ended up in San Diego, California. Fats also moved away that summer, and Carson went along.

Some of the men who split later said they knew Carson wasn't rabid and they were just trying to stop the flight. And Dad, who had stayed with Fats and me in the barn said: "Heck, I knew Carson was okay. He wasn't running, slinking, or growling so I knew he wasn't sick."

He had seen a rabid dog once, and it carried on something fierce until someone shot it. I never had a chance to attend another farm wedding...or any wedding with an ending like that.

1942

Country Christmas 1941

Christmas 1941 came too soon after the Japs bombed Pearl Harbor, Hawaii, and a lot of our neighbors didn't really observe it as a happy time. Every day, what news we were allowed to hear mentioned casualties, and they were all American or Hawaiian. My mother was quieter than usual—she mourned for the casualties and tried to console her brother, who had lost a son during the bombing. We all tried to ignore the fact that my brother Ed would be 18 years old in January of 1942. My dad had obtained a newspaper in Seattle, Washington, that showed some pictures of the bombing of Pearl Harbor and printed something about the magnitude of destruction. We read and re-read that paper several times, basically because it was so hard to believe. It pictured ships burning and airplanes all blown apart. That paper became the topic of all conversation for the month of December.

It was hard to celebrate Christmas after Pearl Harbor...

Usually when December rolled around, my father would bring home a Christmas tree, and we would decorate it with beads, garlands, and strings of popcorn. Then we would place a pretty white star on the top to represent the star of Jerusalem. The tree was usually seven to eight feet tall and almost perfect. In 1941, my father picked up a tree that was only between three and four feet tall, and Mother decorated it with just a few ribbons and a few old Christmas cards she had saved from previous years. Since our house was a quarter of a mile from the county road, we never put up outdoor lights, but we did put up a string of lights around our front room window where the tree stood. It helped cheer us up some.

Almost every year that I can remember, two of our neighbors and our family took turns having a "Dutch lunch" the night before Christmas. For the uneducated, a Dutch lunch consists of sliced, home-canned ham and beef, home-baked rye and whole wheat bread, sliced dill pickles, freshly sliced onions, and fresh churned butter. When it was our turn, Mother would bring out hominy and sauerkraut, all homemade. This year was our neighbor's turn, and we took our big sleigh pulled by our two matched Belgian horses the four miles to the neighbors. We all tried the lunch, and it was good, but the good fellowship was a little diminished for all of the participants. Both of our neighbors had sons who had enlisted in the Navy. I guess they had wanted to see the exotic foreign ports where beautiful young ladies danced with veils on. The sobering aspect of this trend was that, every time a maritime disaster took place, everyone had to wait for the outcome and the list of casualties to be published, and our neighbors would come over to our farm to listen to the radio almost every Wednesday night.

No one even considered a lawsuit...

We used our sleigh in the cold winter months to haul hay and to travel into town to buy provisions when the snow was deepest. Those Belgians had feet like dinner plates and could pull anything anywhere we wanted. We also used the sleigh to visit our neighbors from time to time, which was a lot of fun. Dad always hung a kerosene lantern turned up high on the bottom of the tailgate to serve as a warning to anything coming up behind us that we were there. One night, just before Christmas, we were coming home from town, and the wind was blowing something fierce. My brother and I were lying on the straw bed of the sleigh, covered up with a blanket, and we didn't notice the lantern had been extinguished. All of a sudden, something hit the back of the sleigh, pushing it forward into the horses, and they started to run down the road. It took Dad about a fourth of a mile to get them stopped and calmed down. We climbed out of the sleigh to see what had happened and found one ski broken but usable. After a few minutes, a big green Chevrolet stake truck[1] came slowly to a stop behind the sleigh. It seemed that the trucker, who was hauling a few steers to the auction yards, had run into us at about 30 miles an hour. He said that his lights had quit on the way back from a neighboring ranch, and because our lantern wasn't lit, he couldn't see us. He asked if anyone was hurt, and then said he couldn't stop or leave the truck because of the steers. Dad shook hands with the man and wished him a Merry Christmas. We let the truck pull around our sleigh, and Dad drove on home. There was no mention of right or wrong, and no money changed hands. We got home with Christmas supplies, and the next day my brother fixed the ski.

We all felt lucky even though there weren't many presents...

Christmas came slowly, and instead of a pile of Christmas presents under the little tree, there was only one present for each of us. I told my brother that maybe Santa was overloaded with gifts for everyone but farm kids. He didn't say much except how lucky we all were. We always opened our presents on Christmas Eve after dinner, while Mom and Dad sat and listened to the news on our Atwater-Kent battery radio. We could hear the news too, and it was all bad overseas. We were used to the lunatic in Germany and his crusade to kill everybody in Europe, but none of our friends could understand how a country the size of Japan could confront the great United States of America. Needless to say, the word "Japs" was usually said with an adjective preceding it. That word was usually graphic and totally degrading. Our minister at church prayed for the salvation of Japan. His ending comment was, "Lord, forgive them. They do not have any idea of what they have done."

---

[1] Flatbed truck with stake fence panels around sides for hauling livestock or feed.

Forever etched on my mind...

The year 1941 ended with money still hard to come by, and many farmers were poorer than mice in an empty grain bin. But jobs were starting to open up, and the local factory started to work two shifts, hiring some new workers. Their main production during 1941 was farm machinery, but that rapidly converted to war goods after the dastardly attack by the Japanese at Pearl Harbor. It seemed that, right after Christmas, everyone over 18 was drafted, and all of the farm work fell to the young men and those exempted from service to care for older relatives. The area where I lived seemed to be in a state of inaction until late January of 1942. Then a new beginning seemed to grab hold; we were suddenly in a war economy, and goods began to become hard to find.

The sad Christmas of 1941 is forever etched in my mind. I'll never forget the uncalled-for destruction and waste of lives caused by a bunch of runts on a tiny island. I would hope their actions would never be forgotten by anyone.

1941

Hard Times

Throughout 1939 and 1940 in Floyd County, a whole flock of farmers was somewhat isolated by bad roads, wore out tires, lack of money, and just plain hard times all rolled together. So a bunch of men with automobiles that had good tires and a tank full of co-op gasoline made the rounds of all the farms to not only supply needed products, but also to accumulate as much cash as possible as long as possible.

Our farm was the third farm off Highway 35, and there were 12 farms on north to the county line. I recall many of those gentlemen who called on us, begging for business and selling much needed goods. The following stories are a nostalgic re-cap of days gone by and the hard times encountered.

Traveling salesmen are the same the world over...

I recall the traveling store that came by once a month in an old Model T Ford fitted with a big box on the back of it. The box contained all of the miscellaneous items every farm wife and mother deemed necessary: kitchen gadgets, spices, perfumes, cloth bundles, sewing equipment, candy and gum, soaps, and medical supplies. The salesman did not carry any groceries, and he always left a little bit of good will for the lady of the farm, which included a small sample of makeup and rouge.

He quit painting silos and stuck to barns and chicken coops...

A day or two after that peddler had been to the farm, another salesman in a Model A would drive in to see if we needed anything painted. The side of his car had a sign that said, "Painting—Barns and Silos—Reasonable." He was a nice guy and did a good job, and he always had a bone the size of a large stick for our collie. He only had one fault: he moved slower than the hands on the country school clock, and I never saw him walk faster than Mother's old goose. Besides painting barns so they looked like new, he also did an excellent job painting silos. Dad hired him to paint our old silo, and it took him three days. He rigged up a sling and attached it to the silo, and then he tied a ladder made of rope to the top rung of the silo ladder. On the bottom of the ladder, he tied a swing seat. He would paint about three feet, then move the seat, climb up the rope ladder, re-position the ladder and seat a few more feet around the silo, and paint some more. Each move enabled him to paint a strip about three feet wide and six feet long. Our silo was about 40 feet tall; he painted a good one-third each day, and he did all of the work for $25.00. He said he would paint our barn for $30.00, but Dad said no.

Word got around later that summer that he was painting a silo a few miles north of our farm, when one of the knots let go and dumped him about 12 feet into a pond of silage juice. He wasn't hurt too bad, but after that bath and sucking in some of the vile juice the color of chocolate, he quit painting silos and stuck with barns, hen houses, and out buildings.

The milkman was a critical cog in the wheel…

Another great service that everyone subscribed to was the weekly milk pick-up by the dairy. It employed a route driver to gather the cans from all the farms on the route and deliver them to the dairy for processing. Our driver's name was Willard, and he told me he made about $60.00 a month on the route. Like all farmers, we milked a few cows and kept the milk in five-gallon cans in our spring to keep it fresh. We also had a DeLaval hand crank separator to process some of the milk for cream; we fed the skim milk to our pigs. We always had two or three cans of dairy milk each week. Our route man was known to take a sip or two during his route, and once in a while, he would come into our yard as fast as a swallow chasing bugs. He also sang and chewed some Peerless tobacco, but I never saw him spit. One day he came into the yard and pulled up to the barn in a brand new pickup. It was a Chevrolet and the prettiest truck I had ever seen. I got the chance to look it over while he loaded the milk cans. When he was finished, he came around to the driver's side, climbed in, and grinned at me. He said, "I just went past old Aunt Mary's place, and she told me to tell Tadpole, 'Hello.' I assume you are him, ain't you?" I could tell he had been sipping on something stronger than cider, and when he pulled out of our yard onto the gravel road, he ran right into our neighbor driving by on his Oliver tractor. His new pickup truck ended up in the ditch, but no one was hurt. Another time he pulled into our yard, and I could see milk leaking out of the truck box in a pretty good stream. I told him about it and helped him pick up two five-gallon milk cans that had tipped over and leaked out all of the milk. He looked at me, grinned, and said, "Doggone it, Tadpole! That's a good waste of grow juice, but the cows will surely give up some more to make up for it." I told Dad what had happened, and he thought that Willard would get fired over the loss, but the dairy just made him pay for it.

Shearing sheep and checking for typhoid…

Another service offered was the clipping of sheep for those who kept a few sheep for meat and for a few dollars' income from the wool.

We didn't keep sheep—Dad couldn't stand their bleating all the time—so we had no need for that service. One of the shearers offered to cut my hair for free, but I didn't think he knew how to cut hair.

One morning a state car drove into our farm, and the man driving asked to talk to Dad. I told him that he was gone, so he visited with Mother. I heard the conversation. He asked about our source of water, and when he found out that we used the spring for cooking and drinking, he told us that he wanted to look at the spring. He said that, even though there had been no typhoid in our area, the concern was that the cows and horses could contaminate a water supply and cause problems. He drove up to the spring on the hill, was gone about 30 minutes, came back, and told us that our water supply was in good shape. He said there was no way any animal could get to the spring, what with all of the barbwire, chicken wire, and hog fence around it. He left, and I had the feeling that we were a lot smarter than most of the farmers.

Ben had a loose rivet or two, but he sure sharpened knives...

All summer long, salesmen came to our farm trying to sell everything we didn't need. There was one salesman I'll never forget because we always hired him. He was a little black-headed man who wore high lace-up boots, suspenders, and a small round hat with a turned-up brim that sat on the back of his head. He came to our farm about three times a year, driving an old Model A Ford painted green, with a black top and black wire wheels. Behind his car was a small, two-wheeled trailer fixed to the bumper and covered with canvas. He drove slower than a turtle with a sore toe—real cautious-like—and before he would come to the door, he would uncover the trailer to display a portable grindstone on a frame with a metal seat attached.

He hooked up a small rod to the frame and positioned a one-pound coffee can of oil on it. The can had a hole in the bottom so it would drip oil on the wheel as it turned. When he was ready, he knocked on the door and visited with Mother for a few minutes discussing our neighbors; then Mom would hand him some knives, scissors, and a small hand axe to sharpen. He was a good, polite craftsman and provided a needed service. And the way he went about it almost guaranteed that he would get some work. Mother called him Ben, but his name was Benito Louige Boggio. He spoke with an accent and said he was from Italy. He sang while he worked and had a real good voice. He was always happy. His one bad habit was chewing Beech Nut tobacco. He would peddle the stone real fast, holding the knives just so and spitting off to one side. He would hum and sing in a deep voice about a river in France. The wheel would get hot, and he would stop for a bit, just sitting there. Ben charged 25 cents to sharpen each item, and he got them so sharp they were dangerous to handle.

Dad was home once when he called, and he gave Ben some hook knives used for trimming horse hooves to sharpen. They looked like paring knives with hooked ends. When he was grinding away on the hook knives, he pushed a little too hard and broke the blade off one of the knives right by the handle. In the process, he ground his thumbnail down pretty good and cut his right hand across the palm. Blood squirted, Ben let out a cuss word, and I went and told Mom what had happened. She bandaged up his hand using Cloverine salve, and he apologized for ruining the knife. Mom told him just to throw it away, and everything was okay. He sharpened my old bone-handle knife for free. I thought that maybe he was sipping on corn liquor and maybe had a loose rivet or two, because he was still singing when he left.

Snake oil for animals...

There was another salesman who called on us in 1940. He sold vet supplies and drove a delivery van with shelves on the inside filled with all kinds of cure-alls. He also sold leather scraps for harness repair and had a few buggy whips that he tried to sell. We purchased some of his goods like Liniment and Butter Salve for cows, but the liniment smelled like our silage pit, and Dad never used it. The salesman had a few tools; I thought one was especially neat. It was an awl that punched holes in leather; it was fitted with a curved needle and had a small spool of black thread in the handle so you could sew leather with it. It only cost $1.25, but I never had that much money. He also had a pet ground hog that he kept in a box with sawdust in it that sat on the seat. I thought he was a bit different because we tried to get rid of those critters on our farm.

Maytag washing machines for sale…

One Saturday a small truck drove into our farm and pulled up to the house by the back door. The driver talked with Mom, and then he uncovered the pickup box. Resting there, all tied down with a large rope, was a new Maytag washing machine. It was all white with a red wringer head and a shift lever on the side of the tub to engage the workings of the machine. Dad had bought the latest washing machine made just for farmers who did not have electricity or a generator to provide it. The machine had a small gas engine mounted under the tub to run the agitator and the wringer. There was a small foot pedal to start the engine and a shift lever to begin operation. The wringer head was something new and featured a pressure lever just in case you got something caught that you wanted to release quickly (like your hand). You just pushed the lever, and the rollers parted company and quit rotating.

There was only one caution with the machine—it had to be operated out-doors because of deadly carbon monoxide gas emitted by the engine. We put it on the back porch, and it was used every day. In a day or two, we started to have visitors, who wanted to watch the washer work, especially the rollers.

Long johns were a necessity, plain and simple…

Quite a few kids wore hand-me-down clothes including old coats from older relatives and jeans that were almost threadbare. Some of the farm kids wore shoes with cardboard insoles that had to be changed every night. One little second-grader wore a jacket that was a fugitive from the bon fire. When I told Mother, she sent one of my old jackets for him to wear. Most kids wore long johns for underwear—the kind with the flap in the back—to keep warm.

A few old-timers swore by the custom of bathing just twice a year. Every spring they would peel off their long johns and bathe in the horse tank or the river; then they would put on a new pair of $2.98 cotton long johns and wear them all summer until September.

Then they would do the procedure all over again. Granted, they weren't the best smelling rosebuds in the area, but they never seemed to get pneumonia or any of those old winter afflictions.

Somehow, and I never could figure it out, all the girls always were clean and neat and smelled good in spite of the chores they did and without the benefit of makeup. My desk in school was right behind a young lady named Mary Ann. She always smelled really good, besides being very pretty, but she didn't know I even existed. She always reminded me of a dew-covered yellow rose.

One cold winter day, one of the eighth-grade bullies was teasing some of the girls about wearing long underwear with a seat that buttoned, saying that's what took them so long to go to the outdoor toilet. Miss Heise, our teacher, became madder than a hornet with clipped wings. She rapped her pointer stick on the blackboard, and addressing those men—especially one named Milton—said, "Don't you young gentlemen have any feeling for all of these younger kids? You're supposed to be adults come spring, but I don't see a one of you that will ever wear that label." With that, she lifted her long dress up to her knees and said, "See, I wear long underwear all winter; I'd rather do that than freeze to death." Then she looked right at the eighth-graders and said, "I'll have no more of that kind of teasing." That put a stop to that, and the subject was never mentioned again.

Privies were a fact of life...

The outdoor toilets were a painful necessity, with no heat in the winter and no air conditioning in the summer. Every outdoor "lavatory" had a good supply of books and catalogues for educational reading and other purposes. Sears and Roebuck did a good job of educating a whole lot of farm kids...

Pump salesmen kept the water coming...

The only source of running water on most farms was made possible by a long-handled pump, so there was a water pump salesman who called on us every spring. He helped install pumps free, and they only cost $25.00. Our old pump froze up once, and we purchased a new one from him. He showed us how to prime it and how to shut the drain valve so the leather would stay damp. He was a little odd, in that his shirt was always buttoned one button off, but he didn't seem to mind.

Car salesmen were the same then as now...

Probably the only salesman that wasn't really well-liked was a car salesman who conveyed the impression that he was better than most dirt farmers, so he didn't sell much. This person sold a neighbor a 1933 Packard on credit, and then the crankshaft broke. When the car quit, the neighbor just got out of the car and left it sitting on the road. Nothing ever came of that; the garage just came and towed it home. As the economy improved later on, quite a few farmers bought newer tractors, but continued to run their older model cars, some of which were ready for the junk heap.

During those years, I saw, rode in, and even drove some of those great old cars. There were Essex, Rio, Franklin, Starr, Hudson, Hupmobile, Oakland, Cord, Willies, Knight, Pierce Arrow, Dodge, and Plymouth. I never rode in a Lincoln, Cadillac, or a Packard. But through all those years, Dad drove only Buicks.

Somehow, even with all the trials, tribulations, and salesmen, we all survived, grew up some, and made it through school.

1943

Country Grown Peanuts

World War II was just underway in December of 1941, and everything seemed to change daily. January of 1942 brought newspapers almost entirely saturated with items about the war. Ads for scrap for the war effort started to appear in the paper, and everyone tried to do his or her part. One of the ads in the paper read:

Wanted: Someone to grow and harvest peanuts to be used for the extraction of peanut oil. Very little expense involved as everything will be provided for this opportunity. The press provided will remain the property of the company. Contact: The Medical Oil Company, Attn. Mr. Roberts.

Our neighbor Ted was as easy going as a 30-pound cat with a full stomach. When Ted saw the ad, he came over to our farm and asked me what I thought. I felt a little important because I was only 13 and Ted was about 40. I told him it was probably legitimate, as it had a medical name, and the company was probably part of the war effort. He thought the ad would probably result in a profit for him so he answered the ad. The result of his response was a visit from the mailman who had a package for him. I was over talking to him and was there to watch him open the box. It contained a sack of raw peanuts, a brochure, and a wooden apparatus that looked like my dad's machine vise. Ted read the brochure and looked over the vise.

It sounded like a sure-fire way to get rich...

The brochure stated that the peanuts had to be planted in hills, each hill containing three raw nuts, 12 inches apart and kept well watered. We figured that the "well watered" meant lots of water and not water from a well; in any case, Ted had a good well so that was okay. Each vine would produce more than 20 peanuts, and after the peanuts came off the vine, they were to be collected and shelled into the pan sent with the press. The press was evidently the wooden vise. The shelled nuts had to be denuded of their little brownish coatings and placed in the vise box to be crushed, and the oil caught in a small aluminum jar from a hole in the bottom of the crush board. After all the peanuts were crushed and the oil collected, the oil was to be securely wrapped and sent by mail to the company. Five pounds of peanuts should produce three to five ounces of oil worth

$2.00 an ounce that would be pure profit as there were no expenses except your time and effort.

L to R: Jack Ferguson and Al Anderson, 12 years old, playing horseshoes. Taken around Charles City, Iowa. Summer of 1940.

The darned things grew underground, like potatoes...

I listened carefully, and it sounded like a good project. The letter mentioned vines, so I figured that the nuts grew in bunches and that harvesting them would be duck soup. All you had to do was pick them when they were ripe. I watched as Ted planted the peanuts in his garden, using a small stick to punch little holes for each hill and put three peanuts into each hole. He covered them up, patting the dirt down on each hill. After I helped Ted carry several buckets of well water to put on the hills, he told me that the vines would come up in four or five days.

For about a week, I checked the hills every day, and sure enough, there were dozens of little sprouts poking up through the dirt. We kept them well-watered, and they grew like green pea vines. We checked them daily, but they did not produce any blossoms. One Saturday, Ted checked the vines and, in a fit, pulled up one of the vines. Lo and behold, the darn things grew like potatoes—underground. We pulled the nuts off the vine and cracked them to see what they looked like. We counted 24 on the roots of the vine and then ate them.

After that, every morning when Ted went to the field, I pulled up one vine and harvested the peanuts to save for later. After I had removed about ten vines and accumulated over 200 nuts, Ted told my mother that there was either some animal eating his peanuts or that some bum was raiding his garden. When Mother told me what he said, I admitted that I was the culprit and promised not to do it again. Anyway, I had plenty to eat stashed away.

A few weeks went by, and the vines grew and then began to turn yellow and wither. Frost came late that year, and Ted anticipated a good crop of peanuts. I went over to Ted's house on a Saturday morning, and he had a bushel basket of peanuts sitting on his back step. We sat on the porch for about an hour while Ted read and re-read the instructions included with the press. That press was the darnedest contraption I ever saw. It looked like my dad's vise, but made totally of wood. It was to be mounted on a table, and the inside was to be coated with grease (hog lard) to keep the oil free running as it was squeezed out of the peanuts. The press worked just like a metal vise. The screw and handle were made of hickory, and the rest of it was made of alder. There were sides on the slide box to hold the nuts, and there was a small hole in the bottom of the back board to let the peanut oil drain into the container.

One-fourth of a pint of oil is not much of a harvest…

We got the vise mounted on the table, and Ted threw a handful of peanuts into the squeeze box. We grabbed the wooden screw handle and turned it to move the nuts back towards the crushing board. He turned it as far as he could, and we looked into the small tank used to catch the oil. It was bone dry, like a parched throat in the middle of August. Not one drop of oil came out. We decided to call the medical company for help. When I went over to Ted's the next day, he told me what we had done wrong. He said that any oil squeezed out of the peanuts was soaked up by the crushed shells and the little skins on the nuts. He said we had to take off the shells and pick off the little brown skins from the peanuts before we pressed them.

Ted and I spent the next day shucking and cleaning the peanuts. On the following Saturday, we got together and filled up the press, and Ted worked the handle. We checked the little container, and sure as heck, there was about a teaspoon of oil in the jar. We worked all that Saturday, shelling, cleaning, and pressing the oil out of the nuts. We ended up with about one-fourth of a pint of oil. We followed instructions, packaging the oil in a small aluminum can with a glass top. Ted wrapped it in butcher paper and packed it real good in a shoebox. He mailed the package with the rural mailman, first class delivery.

About five days later, a big, black Nash automobile pulled into Ted's yard. I saw it coming and ran over to see what was going on. I sat on the porch and listened as hard as I could. I didn't hear all that was said, but I heard enough to know it was about the peanut oil. After a while, two men left in the car, and Ted came out of the house. He sat down on the porch, looked at me, and grinned.

All I have left is two pennies behind the fuses in the kitchen…

He said, "Kid, I've had more trouble than a math teacher who don't know how to add. A few years ago, I made a down payment on this run-down old farm and brought my bride here to make a home. She was a beautiful lady with a smile like a string of pearls, but she had a temper like a one-legged sailor with the gout."

I didn't know what that was, but I kept listening.

"My wife up and left me in the middle of the night. My bull croaked right after that, and what corn I had burned up in a grass fire. I bought that old Model A sitting out there, and after I got it home, it never would run again. I owe everybody, and I hoped to make a few dollars out of this peanut thing. Now I just found out that the peanut oil I sent to the oil company never got there. The mail car on the train evidently threw something on top of it, and it got crushed. The oil leaked out and ran all over the mail in the sack. Some of it was official mail, and someone thought it was sabotage. That darned oil sure got me in a lot of trouble. The only money I've got is the two pennies I put behind the fuses[2] in the kitchen."

Everybody had troubles during that time...

I sat with him for a while and then went home feeling bad. A couple of days later, Ted got a letter from the medical oil company demanding the press back and a payment of $100 for destruction of mail. About one week later, I went to see Ted, but he was gone. The old car was still there, and in the house were a few apple boxes and an old bare bed. I never saw him again. The banker came and put a lock on the gate, telling me to watch out for thieves. I don't know why, because there was nothing to steal. Later on, as I grew up, I thought about Ted and his problems. Everybody had problems during that time—Ted just ran away from his. I sent the press back.

1947

Country Justice

One day in July of 1941, my dad told my brother Ed to bring in our roan cow to the holding pen so the new owner could load her into his truck. Dad had sold her to a neighbor for butchering. Ed saddled up a horse and rode out to haze her into the pen. He spent quite a while bringing her in, and I helped by closing

---

[2] Placing a penny in the fuse socket allowed the power to bypass the rating of the fuse, and although it was commonly done, it was risky business.

the gate. She was the most miserable animal we had, and I was glad to see her go. She was meaner than a hung-over bull rider and would charge anyone she saw. I had seen her chase Billy, our old pet goat, and knock him head-over-heels more than once. I was deathly afraid of her, but Ed said he could handle loading her into the truck. He went to get a pitchfork, and when he returned with it, he remarked that most animals are scared of a fork. I'd heard that baloney before when we had the escapade with Blackie, the bull. Ed should have learned from that, too, but he hadn't.

He ran up the ramp with the cow right behind...

We waited by the loading ramp for Fred, the farmer who had bought the cow. About a half an hour later, he drove into the barnyard and backed up to the loading ramp. That red cow stood watching us by the ramp, and I thought she was going to charge the truck. The pickup was equipped with a stock rack that swung away from the tailgate, and all I had to do was drop the tailgate. Ed took the pitchfork and stepped into the holding pen, poking the pitchfork at the cow. From what I could see, the cow didn't blink or move as Ed got closer. When he was about ten feet away, the roan cow bawled out something that sounded obscene and started for Ed. He dropped the fork and ran up the ramp with the cow right behind. He jumped into the pickup box and vaulted right over the cab, yelling at me to shut the tailgate. As the cow went into the pickup box after Ed, I slammed the tailgate shut and closed the stock rack. I looked for Ed, and he was standing over by the barn. The cow butted the back of the pickup cab a few times and then settled down. Ed told Fred that the cow was meaner than all get out. He said she hated everyone.

Later, I asked Ed why he didn't prod the cow into the pickup like we always did. He said he figured having her chase him was the easiest way to load her. I looked at Mom, and she just smiled. She told us that she was glad the cow was gone. When Dad came home a few days later, he asked how the sale went. My mother said it was an exercise in perseverance, teamwork, and agility. I think Ed was the happiest of all that the cow was gone.

Misrepresentation and assault and battery by complicity...

On August 28, my birthday to officially be 13 years old, a deputy sheriff drove into the yard and handed Mother a summons. I had never seen one of those, and I asked what it was. She finished reading the letter and told me that Dad had to appear in court to answer some charges. Fred had charged Dad with a long list of sins: misrepresentation, assault and battery by complicity, hospital costs, and loss of income, as well as compensation for mental anguish and suffering. He was to appear to 9:30 a.m. on the following Tuesday to respond to the charges.

It seems that Fred had transported the roan cow home and had planned to unload her into a small pen where he kept his calves at night. The long ride to her new home had banged the cow around pretty good, and her temperament was that of an enraged elephant. According to Fred, he was unaware of her crotchety disposition, and he swore under oath that he thought she was a sweet and gentle milk cow—one of those that stood around chewing her cud, chasing flies with her tail, and waiting to be milked. He thought he would back the pickup up to the pen and open the tailgate, and she would meander out to look over her new home. Fred said he did just that, but when he dropped the tailgate, she jumped right at him and knocked him over into a water tank next to the gate. He told the judge that the cow hit him so hard he almost drowned before he could get out of the tank. He said he thought the cow was just eager to exit the truck, and it was an accident that she almost killed him.

The Judge asked Fred if anyone had told him that the cow was ornery as a loco steer, and Fred said no. He then told the judge that, as he climbed out of the water tank, the cow tried to gore him, and he fell back into the tank. He tried to catch himself and pulled his right arm out of its socket. He said he was able to climb out of the back side of the tank and had carefully walked over to his truck to drive it out of the pen. He was almost in the truck, all but his left leg, when the cow rammed the door with a full head of steam. That was when he broke his left leg below the knee. He stated that he was in great pain, and only had the use of one leg and one arm to get out of the pickup. He headed for the house and fell several times, causing terrible pain and anguish. He said it took over an hour before his wife could get him to the hospital, and he suffered so bad he almost died.

When he got to the hospital, they cut off his left boot, which was brand new and had cost him 50 bucks. He said he spent four days in the hospital after they put a cast on his leg. He had to lie in bed with his left leg raised up on a trolley to keep it still. He wasn't able to chew tobacco for four days, and a nurse shoved a cold bedpan under him every few minutes. He was humiliated to be in such a horrific position. He blamed it all on Dad for not telling him the cow might bust him up if he wasn't careful. He said that he just knew that "the engineer" knew the cow would do what she did, and that Dad was getting even with him for Dad's fence having been cut a year ago, necessitating our cows to be rounded up from down along the river.

Fred asked the judge for compensation of $600 for all of his bills, suffering, and laid-up non-productive time. In those days, $600 was about six months' wages, and he figured that amount would cover everything.

Back when judges administered justice...

Dad sat and listened during all of Fred's testimony and never said a word. When the judge asked him to tell his side, Dad told the following: "Judge, I never knew until now who cut my fence and stole one of our calves. I do now. I know that Fred had seen the old roan cow several times and wanted her to produce a few roan calves for him. He begged me to sell her to him for butcher, and I did. He never asked about her disposition or if she was mean and ornery like most older bovines. She had just produced a beautiful roan calf five months before he took her home. She had never attacked me (he was gone quite a bit), and I was never in the holding pen when she was there. I have never lied to sell any animal—cow, horse, sheep, or pig, not even a gopher—period. My son told Fred that she was dangerous."

Looking at Fred, Dad said, "As for loss of income, Fred, when was the last time you got out of your pickup to do anything but eat, drink, or sleep? Your wife does all of the work around your place, even the plowing. If it weren't for your neighbors, you wouldn't have a place to steal chickens or eggs for meals. Hell, a fox is more of a neighbor than you; at least we know when he's in the hen house stealing. As for mental anguish, you've never worried about anything but getting to town for commodities, which are free. And your bath in the water tank was probably number one this year, according to what your wife told mine."

I didn't understand everything Dad told the judge, but the answer from the judge was plain and simple. He looked at Fred and said, "There is no case here. I find no complicity, misrepresentation, or assault and battery. Case dismissed."

Needless to say, we were not friends after that, and it was surprising how fast Fred healed up. He later sold his rundown farm and moved away. The roan cow stayed with the place and was there when we moved to another farm clear across the county. I missed the old man when we didn't have any one else to worry about.

1947

Country Style Thanksgiving

Thanksgiving in the country was a great event, especially for kids, basically because of the four-day vacation. In anticipation of the great holiday, the whole month of November dragged slowly by, sitting in that one-room schoolhouse trying to learn with so many distractions coming up. Even an occasional chew of Beechnut chewing tobacco while playing with a tiny turtle kept in your lunch box, or occasionally holding a small green frog that was kept in the bib overall pocket in a damp handkerchief didn't make the time go faster.

On Wednesday before Thanksgiving, all of our neighbors attended a Thanksgiving play at the country school. There were over 30 people in attendance. It gave us boys a chance to ignore all of the girls and walk around like we owned the school. My school heartthrob Mary Jane told my buddy Fats that I was the dumbest, ugliest kid in the school. I knew she was trying to trap me, and I told Fats he could have her, on the condition that he didn't dunk her hair in the inkwell or put tacks on her chair. I even shared some Juicy Fruit gum with him, but Fats decided that he didn't want to get hitched yet and declined my gift. After the school activities ended, school was let out for four days vacation. It was like being paroled, as we could lie around and eat and play in the haymow of our barn.

Line School Students. North of Charles City, Iowa. 1943.
Back Row L to R: Al Anderson, Verle Miller, Evelyn Anderson, Emil Zimmerman, Miss Heise, teacher, Emil's sister, and Joyce Miller.
Front Row L to R: Fred Wagner, Frank (unknown last name), Janice Miller, Willets boy and girl, and John Anderson.

Girlfriends were expensive, especially a passel of them...

Usually in November, the snow piled up deep and cold, and the walk of one mile or more to school almost froze your ears solid. And to top that off, the big wood-burning, pot-bellied heating stove never seemed to get the chill out of the room. Most of the pupils wore long underwear and sweaters while at school, and even our teacher wore unmentionables under heavy clothing, and how we found that out will never be revealed.

My older brother had a passel of girlfriends—more than a caterpillar has legs. I used to watch him make out little cards with Thanksgiving blessings on them, and pile them up nice and neat in  alphabetical order so he didn't miss anybody. All the time he was doing this, he complained about being so popular. The cards cost about five cents apiece, and he went through at least 20 at Thanksgiving and Christmas. The stamps cost one cent each, which caused Ed to remark that the cushy job most postmen had didn't warrant paying them 15 cents an hour. Ed evidently forgot the times his letters were delivered in three feet of snow and drifts, many times by sleigh.

Ed told me that he was going to give up all of his girlfriends from the end of September until December 31, and he would save tons of money. He said he thought that they would still remember him with a present or two because he had treated them so good in the past.

Dinner that would make a Roman orgy seem like a tea party...

Preparing for the trip to church for Thanksgiving was a real chore. It seemed like it took forever to take a bath in the large galvanized washtub, using water heated on a stove in pans, and using soap that could peel the shell off a black walnut. But once clean, you felt terrific, and you knew you were ready for anything. Dad and Mom would load all of us kids and Ed—Ed wasn't considered a kid—into the family car, and off to church we would go. Mother always sat in the back seat, and we all crowded in the front and back of the car. Sometimes we'd sing songs like *The Old Rugged Cross* or maybe *What a Friend We Have in Jesus* entirely off-key, but creating the feeling of well-being. And I'm sure the organist at the church really looked forward to all of us off-key singers...

During the Thanksgiving observance, the preacher would extol the virtues of generosity towards others (could have been for himself) and usually gave an impassioned sermon. When the collection plate was passed, it always ended up full to the brim, even though most of us were short of money. After church, we headed home for a dinner that would have made a Roman orgy seem like a casual tea party. My mother always spent the previous day baking, mixing, and cooking, and the old farmhouse smelled so good it made everyone's mouth water, including our shepherd, Sandy.

The odor of roasting turkey drove Amos wild...

Dad would bring the turkey in to be de-feathered and prepared for its rightful place at the center of the table. I kind of missed those huge red, white, and black birds and their music for two or three days afterwards, but like my dad always said, "You can't have a turkey and a dinner too."

Our dog and cat usually sat by the kitchen door, drooling on each other and letting out an occasional yelp or loud meow, before we left for church. Mother would put the gigantic turkey in the oven to slowly cook and fill the house with the smells of holiday. We couldn't wait to get home to really enjoy Thanksgiving. As soon as we arrived home from church, our dog Sandy parked by the dining room door in anticipation of some turkey and gravy with mashed potatoes on the side.

Mother had an orange-striped tomcat named Amos that had five toes on each paw. He weighed about 30 pounds bone-dry before lunch. On Thanksgiving, he brought a dead mouse into the house and dropped it at my mother's feet as a present. The odor of roasting turkey almost drove him wild, and you could hear him purr for about 50 feet. He always followed my mother around the house on Thanksgiving, purring and meowing like mad.

One time, Mother opened the door to remove the roaster, and Amos tried to climb into the oven. When his two feet hit the oven pan, he let out a sound like a treed mountain lion with a bad foot, jumped backwards, and dashed out the pet door cut into the kitchen screen door. The last I saw of him, he was streaking for the barn like a striped beach ball on legs. Ed and I laughed, but Mother made us go get him so she could put some Cloverine salve on his paws.

I fell totally in love at first sight, again…

Another time, my brother drove off to town Thanksgiving morning and returned just before noon in Dad's new Buick. He had a passenger with him, and when he stopped by the front door, out stepped one of the prettiest ladies I had ever seen. She had on blue jeans, a shirt with pearl snaps, and a blue handkerchief on her long brown hair. She was as pretty as a movie star, and I fell totally in love at first sight, again. It didn't help any when Ed told me he had given up all of his other girlfriends for her. Her name was Marjorie, and I remembered her face for a long time after he took her home. It was pure hell to be only 13 years old and only able to sneak looks at her all day long.

Ed's romance was short-lived, though, when her dad found them kissing in our car that night and told Ed where the bear trampled in the buckwheat.

The next day, Ed relented and sent all of his other girlfriends small Christmas cards.

For four days, we had dreaded the coming Monday when school took back up, but there was a good future ahead. Christmas was coming in about one month, with its two weeks of time off for good behavior, and hopefully, some real neat presents under the Christmas tree. There was just one big problem: this was the last family Thanksgiving until next year.

1947

The Model A

I'll never forget that summer day
When Dad brought home the Model A.
With canvas top and wire feet,
A hump-backed coupe with rumble seat,
Made by Ford and painted green,
The prettiest car I'd ever seen.

An Armstrong starter beneath its nose,
A spark advance on the steering post,
A lighted dash and a corkscrew jack,
With a tire kit to fix a flat.
"It's the latest thing," I heard him say,
"Made in Detroit, it's a Model A."

A round Ford sign was on the shroud,
And Dad stood by looking proud,
"Look her over; I'm sure you'll agree,
It's a better car than our Model T.
It runs real good on these country roads,
And you can bet she really goes."

She had a shifting lever on the floor,
And wedge type locks to hold each door,
A windshield wiper on the driver's side,
And a rumble seat that opened wide,
A rubber mat beneath your feet,
And a heater that really threw off heat.

Looking back, I can still recall
That first new car we owned that fall.
How proud we drove her into town,
Mom up front with the top pulled down.
I'll never forget that summer day,
'Cause we lived years with that Model A.

1952

County Polyticks

During the hard times of the late Thirties, politicians weren't too popular with most of the farmers and ranchers that I knew. Dislike for office holders and/or seekers became the topic of conversation at most area get-togethers I attended with my family. Actually, the only community leaders who were cheerfully tolerated were the welfare director and the head of the surplus commodity section of the agriculture department.

Commodities were a selection of non-perishable food items deemed surplus by the government, and they were given from long-term storage to those that needed help to survive. Two of the staples were corn meal and flour, albeit with protein in the form of bugs from being in storage facilities for a lengthy term. One of the best items was cheese, and almost everyone had a good-sized hunk in the kitchen for cooking. There was a variety of other commodities given out: honey, sugar, potatoes, and once in a while, bacon. All that was required for a family to receive commodities was to be dirt poor, apply at the commodity office, and swear they would not trade, sell, or otherwise dispose of the free food. They had to accept everything on the list and sign their name and address indicating they had received everything. Quite a few sacks of flour and corn meal ended up at the local dump because they were unpalatable—there were other ways to find protein besides eating it in their commodities. The CCC men usually traded for part of the cheese; because they were a big help to the rural population, they were well-liked by everyone.

"Polyticking" usually began in the spring of the election year, after the weather broke and while everyone was still hopeful for prosperity that was always "just around the corner." That corner seems to have been five or six years long… To top that off, country roads were a nightmare in most areas, and horses were a godsend clear up and into May of each year. Some cars got bogged down, causing other vehicles to get stuck, and farmers were kept busy extracting cars at $1 a car.

In some instances, trying to unseat an office holder from the gravy train dining car and getting people to vote for a newcomer was extremely hard to do. Slurs, innuendos, and outright slander were used—especially by someone who planned to oust an office holder and take his place. The politicians came, car after car, some in Levis and Stetsons, and some in store-bought suits with shoes so shiny they were like mirrors. Those with store-bought teeth had a way of flashing big toothy grins as they opened their car door, sticking their hands out from ten feet away, and introducing themselves in a loud voice. If you were not too cautious and shook their hands, you were treated to a good ten-minute speech as your hand was pumped up and down.

Dad took to keeping his right hand in his pocket whenever anyone drove into our yard. His excuse was a sprained wrist from handling too many loads of manure. The surprising thing was that all the politicians knew every farmer and rancher in the area and their wives and kids, and they threw the names around trying to convince everyone that they were good old boys and should be elected to office. After the election was over, you never saw them again, and if you did, they didn't seem to know who you were. When we attended church, we would see a few elected politicians who were always in a hurry to leave.

Dad called politicians "Baloney Spreaders" because they were all full of baloney. He did support the county commissioners, because they kept all of the county roads clear and passable year 'round. He said that most of the rest just wanted a cushy job so they could relax and not strain themselves like the rest of the working men did. I remember some of the situations that occurred, and I wrote them in my notebook for the future. I was only 12 in 1940, but I used to stand by my dad and listen to the conversations and the promises that some of the candidates made. Each one had his own cause and promises that he knew he couldn't keep. Some promises were so far out they sounded ridiculous and didn't apply to rural families. And, of course, the politicians never had anything to say that was good or positive about their opponents. Dad always said that our Founding Fathers made too many takers and not enough givers.

He was just a starving lawyer looking for a better job...

I've listed some of the conversations that took place in our front yard. They will bring back memories of those bygone days when almost anything was said or done to win an election. The first politician I kept track of drove into our farm in an almost new 1939 Ford Sedan Touring Car. It was all shiny, black as shoe polish, and had tires with real wide white sides on all four wheels. He parked under our big elm tree and crawled out of the car carrying a black leather zip-up case in his left hand, smiling through white teeth that I didn't think were really his. He was dressed in a black suit and had a little round hat on that Dad later called a bowler hat. His shoes really shined, and he smelled like he had been dipped in lilac perfume. He approached us with his right hand outstretched for about ten feet. Dad shook his hand, and the man wouldn't let go. He told Dad his name was Franklin, and he was going to be County Treasurer and would appreciate our vote for him in the fall. He expounded at length on the shortcomings of the existing treasurer, and how he would do a much better job and save all the poor rural taxpayers a bundle of tax money.

I listened to all the reasons the current treasurer shouldn't have even been elected in the first place. He was inefficient, employed too many clerks (all of them younger ladies), was mean-spirited to all those old folks who were late in paying their taxes, and always had lunch in a café. He was also too old, walked bent over, and was too friendly with the sheriff. He was a shyster, and it was surprising that he hadn't been caught in some underhanded scheme. He had divorced his hard-working wife and tied the knot with a young filly about half his age that had black hair and wore high-heeled shoes. Franklin said he would change everything, if we would just help him oust the man out of office. Franklin felt that he deserved to win because he liked old people and went to church quite a bit.

Dad told me later that he knew the Treasurer and that everything Franklin said was a bunch of baloney. Franklin was a lawyer who was starving to death, and he was desperate.

He admitted he was one hell of a good sheriff...

The next tooth-full grin belonged to the County Sheriff. He came driving up in an older Chevrolet that was all muddy and needed a good cleaning so you could see the county markings on the doors. He caught Dad at home just as he was leaving to go to work, and Dad was in a hurry. The sheriff shook Dad's hand and asked for his vote. He didn't criticize anyone, but he did admit that he was one hell of a good sheriff and really enforced the law. He said he hoped that Dad had forgiven him for the traffic violation the year before—driving a tractor on a county road with no lights at all. Dad didn't say anything—I guess he did remember the cost of the ticket—but he walked off, telling the sheriff he had to go to work.

After Dad left, the sheriff asked me if I had seen anything out of the ordinary in the area, like lots of cars coming and going, and if I had noticed any strange odors in the area. I told him that the only odors I had noticed was Mom's cooking, and it always smelled good. I also told him that the only car I had seen lately belonged to a man named Franklin, and he wanted to be the new treasurer. After the sheriff left, I told Mom what he had asked, and she just smiled. I thought that the oversized red nose the man had wasn't caused by NOT drinking some of the corn whiskey that was made in the area. I had the feeling that the sheriff was looking to buy and not arrest.

Two spiels for one...

The next two baloney spreaders came in the same car. One wanted to be the County Assessor, and the other man, to be the County Commissioner. Dad was gone so they gave me two pamphlets with all of their good qualifications listed and told me to tell Dad to vote for them. The County Commissioner aspirant lived just down the road, and I knew Dad would vote for him; it was one way of keeping our road open year around. I wasn't too sure about the other man; he didn't act friendly, didn't talk much, and chewed tobacco and spit on the front wheel of his car.

Vote for ME for Public Instructor...

A few more candidates came by, one of them a lady who drove up in an older Ford car and almost clipped our tree. She came up to the house to see my mother, and I think she was trying to be a Public Instructor for the rural district. They talked for quite a while, and she seemed real nice. As she climbed back into her car, she told me to tell Mom to vote for the best person, "Me!" Her hair was redder than a cowboy's eyes after a three-day drunk.

Just tell why you were sued twice and how you won both suits...

The last one to come to our home was all business; he wanted to be an Attorney for the County. Dad was home, and they talked. I heard Dad ask him why he had been sued twice, and both times, the legal action was a joke and he had won both suits. All that the lawyer said was that everyone had to follow procedural law, innocent or guilty. I'm sure Dad never voted for him. Our laws are great, but those who use them should have ethics and not abuse them.

That fall in the middle of September, our family attended a picnic sponsored by the local Oliver and Allis-Chalmers dealers. Those two dealers furnished everything for the picnic. I knew that every farmer and rancher in the area had some of the equipment sold by both dealers. I happened to see the County Treasurer sitting with Franklin, and I told Dad about it. He just said, "Birds of a feather flock together." It was sure funny how those smiling buggers who degraded those in office became just like them, if they were elected.

Finally, the polyticking was over...

I was happier than a new colt on a summer morning when the election was over. Franklin won and never even thanked the voters for electing him. The sheriff was re-elected; he came by and thanked Dad for his vote. The redheaded lady was defeated, and Mom told me it probably had something to do with her hennaed hair, whatever that meant. And the County Commissioner who lived on our road was elected and put a small "Thank You" ad in the local paper. After all the political commotion was over, everything on our farm kept going on as usual with no major catastrophes. Even our chickens continued to work hard to provide breakfast and Sunday dinner without going on strike. We were all looking forward to Thanksgiving and Christmas, all the time wishing the war would end soon.

Dad's remark to me the day after the election was that we should put all of the politicians in a boat, head it off to Japan, and let them talk the Japs into a quick surrender. He said the Japs had three options if we did that: first, sink the boat; second, surrender; or third, put them all in jail. No matter what the Japs decided, we'd be rid of them, and the war might be over.

1942

Future Farmers of America—Maybe

When country school came to a close in May of 1941, the older kids who attended the crossroads school in Floyd County were given the opportunity to participate in a program that was supposed to bring more city folks out to the farms so they could see what farming was all about. Those of us who had friends in Charles City, Iowa, could invite kids in the same age group to spend the day observing and helping with chores and copying a farm kid's normal day. In that way, they could see just what farming was about and see what an easy time farm kids had. I figured that whoever dreamed that sentence up was either a complete stranger to farming, slightly drunk, unbalanced, or had trouble with the truth.

Dad told Ed and me to give it our best effort, and if only one kid became a farmer, we would be successful. We wrote down the names of several kids who would benefit from the experience and planned to have some of them come out. After spending Saturday experiencing the easy and slow farm life, they would stay the night and leave after breakfast on Sunday. I figured that I was going to let the unlucky visitor just follow me around and pray for an early bedtime.

Ed told me the most outrageous lies, but Mother just smiled...

I was almost growed up, and I could do anything required to keep the farm in good condition. I had learned from my brother Ed

111

that, if force was ever used, a punch in the eye would only hurt for a bit so I had to give it all I had if someone picked a fight—no matter where I was. Ed was tough as nails and had never lost a fistfight.

Ed also had the biggest array of girlfriends, who all thought he was the handsomest 18-year-old in Floyd County. He was always egging me on to latch onto a cute little girl and take her to the show some night. I told him that, if he would lend me the money, I would do just that and buy her some popcorn to munch on, too. That usually kept him off my back, because his array of ladies kept him broke.

Every time Ed came driving into the yard with a new girlfriend, it seemed that she had more arms than an octopus. She would have her arms wrapped around his neck so tight he had a hard time steering his car. The friend that he brought out to spend the day not only had him all wrapped up but also had an arm hanging out the passenger side window. I had asked Ed if all of his lady friends had more than two arms, and he replied, "You sure are a nit wit; most girls' arms are elastic and can stretch. It makes them more cuddly." I was only 11 in 1939, but I knew that no one, not even Ed's friends, had arms that stretched out. Whenever my mother heard Ed telling me those outrageous lies, she would smile and shake her head at him. Ed's lady friends seemed to enjoy his nonsense, and they would smile at me as if to say, "That's baloney—or worse!"

The last Sunday in July of 1939, Ed went to Nashua and attended the Little Brown Church to pick up his first visitor. Her name was Edith, and he had told me that she was as pretty as a new colt. She had brown hair, blue eyes, and freckles all over her cheeks. Ed never lied to me about his friends. This time he had chosen a real winner, and she was openly friendly and fit right in on our farm. Ed came slowly into the yard and parked his car down by our corncrib. When he shut it down, the darn car kept running and emitting clouds of blue smoke. When it finally did quit running, they climbed out of the car, and Ed gave Edith a grand tour of our farm. When they were done with the tour, Edith went into the house to visit with Mother and help in any way she could.

Ed came over to the front porch and sat down. I asked him why he had shown her the evil-smelling chicken coop, the horrible pigsty, and the uncleaned barn. He said, "It's good for every visitor to realize that farming is a hard, odiferous, and dirty job and not one for the squeamish or the sissies."

I had to agree because I was the one who had to clean the chicken coop, the pigpens, and the barn. Cleaning the chicken coop was the worst job on any farm, and nothing smelled so utterly disgusting as a dirty chicken coop. After Ed took Edith home, he came over to the porch, and we talked about his plans to go to the University of Minnesota. He said he didn't want to be a farmer with kids, debt, and all of the hard work involved on a farm. Then he stood up and said, "Let's go clean out the pig pens."

Helping people sometimes paid good dividends...

Cleaning out the sty was a real sickening chore, but it had to be done. The fat, lazy pigs walked around grunting and trying to pick fights, or else they laid down in the dirtiest and muddiest part of the pen that had an odor I can't describe. When I let them out to run while we cleaned the area, they all raced over to our silo and flopped right down in the ring of juice around the silo base. Ed told me that that area was a health spa for them.

One Saturday, as Ed helped me clean up the pens, he asked me if I had seen the spotted boar mixing in with our white pigs. I said they were so covered with mud that I hadn't even noticed the odd ball. Then I mentioned that the farmer over by the crossroads school had a bunch of pigs colored like Holstein cows. We jumped into Ed's Chevy and drove over to the school, laying down a pretty good fog of gas and oil smoke. Right across from the school, we saw a whole bunch of pigs colored black and white. Ed spotted the farmer by the open barn door, so Ed pulled right up to him and asked him if he was missing an old, spotted boar from his herd of pigs.

The farmer's name was Si Roberts, and he was about 70 and slow moving. He studied Ed for a moment and then said, "Yah, I knew that old bugger was gone, but I figured that someone had borrowed him to use as a breeder."

When Ed told Si that we had his boar in with our pigs, he said, "Holy Joseph. How did he get the couple of miles down to your farm?"

Ed told him that we were the only other farm with pigs on the road, and that his boar had probably heard and spotted our squealing porkers and just walked into the yard and joined our animals. Ed said the boar had made himself right at home and was probably looking for female companionship. Si sent his wife down the next day, and we loaded the pig into their new pickup, where he really made himself to home.

The next afternoon Si's better half drove into our yard and handed Ed a good-sized apple pie to thank us for our trouble. It was really delicious, but not as good as Mother's. It seemed to me that honesty and helping people sometimes paid good dividends.

All city kids should take a class on farming...

Our next visitors came from Charles City. A lot of friends of my folks seem to think that our farm was a holiday spot and that they should be treated with great care. We were stuck with some throughout the summer that didn't know a bull from a cow, and once they left the city limits, they were totally dependent on our family to get them through until Saturday. I have to admit that the whole summer was a real burden on my family.

One Saturday, one of Mother's friends came driving into the yard, and out popped this homely little runt that she intended to leave until Sunday. I told him to go and look around, but not to open any gates or go into any animal pens unless I was with him. A bit later, I saw him standing by the chicken coop and just watching them scratch for bugs. I figured that would keep him out of trouble for a while, so I left and filled up a pail of shelled corn. I left the pail of corn by the coop while I went to the barn. When I came out of the barn, I caught him in the act of throwing whole corn into the chicken pen. I explained to him that chickens couldn't eat whole corn. He looked at me and said, "You're lying. They're eating the corn." I told him that chickens do not have teeth and that they have to be fed what their gizzard[3] can grind up so they can get nutrition.

_____

[3] The gizzard contains gravel which works with stomach muscles to grind up food.

114

The preceding conversation led to a whole series of questions, which I answered as truthfully as I could. I finally told him to find a book about chickens at the library when he got back to town and to shut up and go see his mother. He was not very well-versed on farm animals, especially chickens. The kid ran to the house and told his mother that I was picking on him. I was reprimanded for not being patient with a prospective future farmer. I just kept my mouth shut. I later told Mom that all city kids should take a class on farming, so they would know where their food came from: from a farmer to the store and then to their table.

Never, never try to explain breeding to a little town girl...

Another time a friend brought her little daughter with her, and I was told to show her around. The second we got outdoors, the little darling struck out at me and said, "You look like a big sissy to me. Why don't you ride one of those big cows in the pen behind the barn?" I told her that those two animals were bulls and not cows. She asked me if they were bull cows, and what did they do on the farm? Then I made one humongous and almost fatal mistake; I told her that their farm use was for breeding purposes. She asked me why they were "bleeding," and I realized that I was in real deep trouble. I just sent her in to ask her mother that question.

It was just a few minutes until I was called into the house. I tried to think of a way out of the situation, but I knew that I was cornered and that I shouldn't have said what I did. I walked up to the kitchen door, and there stood the little angel, with her thumb in her mouth. Her mother was scowling with her hands on her hips, Mom standing behind them. I could see that her mother was ready to fight, but Mom wasn't upset at all.

The little tattletale pointed at me and said, "The two big cows in the pen next to the barn were both bleeding, and he was the one responsible for it." Her mother looked at me and said, "Why are they bleeding? Did you hurt them?"

I drew a deep breath and thankfully said, "No, ma'am, they were hurt."

She digested that and, turning to her daughter, told her that the poor cows were okay and that she should go out and play until they were ready to leave. I told the little girl that I was sorry I had let the cows get hurt. She followed me outside and went towards the barn. She stopped at the holding pen to stare at the cows (bulls) as I entered the barn. I went into the barn, dashed out the back door, and hid in Dad's 1927 Oakland stored in the shelter shed. I didn't come out until our company had driven out of the yard.

Those city kids just ruined our summer...

Summer after summer, the visits went on, and a few of the visits caused hard feelings between our families. It seems that, although they expected preferential care, we were supposed to let them "do their own thing" on the farm. One Saturday a man, who worked for the Oliver Company and knew Dad, dropped off his 12-year-old son to spend the day. That was the worst day of the summer for me. As I watched, a young city-bred kid exited the car and stood watching the car leave. I had the feeling the kid had been dumped onto other farms before. He walked over to our big oak tree and sat down. He had on a white sweatshirt with a big pocket on the front. He pulled a candy bar out of the pocket, tore the wrapper off, and tossed the crumpled paper on the ground. He ate the candy and just sat leaning on the tree.

I was 12 years old, too, and about the same size as this new kid. I walked over to him and asked his name. He told me that his "moniker" was Fredrick Brown and that his dad was a foreman at the Oliver Plant—or as he put it—a big cheese at the Hart-Parr Company. Since we had just bought an Oliver Row Crop 66 tractor, he looked it over good and seemed to settle right into the farm. He appeared to be a tough little bugger, but I told him to pick up the candy wrapper. He said, "If you want it picked up, pick it up yourself."

I didn't take too kindly to his attitude, and I knew I had the making of a hard day ahead. I looked him in the eyes and said, "You've got a choice: pick up your garbage or I'll whip your pretty jacket right off you."

He continued to sit there for a few moments and then slowly got up, picked up the paper, and stuck it into his pocket. I just knew, though, that he would throw it away the first chance he got.

I didn't want him following me around so I told him to just look around and I'd be back in a little while to work with him. I went out to the barn and watched him from a window. He ambled over to the pigpen and watched the pigs squeal and root around in the mud, and then he went over to the cow pen and watched the cows and the two bulls in the pen. They were pawing up the dirt and grunting at each other in a mock fight. Then I watched Fred while he climbed over the gate and jumped down into the pen with the bulls.

Fred said he was just going to pet the bulls...

I ran out of the barn and yelled at him to get out of there before he got killed. He didn't even look at me or ask me why. I knew he was in deep trouble. Even our old collie stood by the fence barking at the idiot. Even he knew that kid shouldn't be in that pen. The worst scenario would be that he would be trampled and gored. I ran and got my older brother, and Ed broke any record he had getting to the pen, grabbing a three-tined pitchfork on the way. He yelled at the kid to slowly walk to the gate. The kid shouted back, "Why should I? I'm going to go pet those cows."

That's when I heard Ed use words that would have got me a real good "razor-strap licking." I rounded out my vocabulary that day with words I'd never heard before.

Fred was standing about ten feet away from the gate and 60 feet from the bulls. They were carrying on something fierce, and I expected to see them charge the kid any minute. I knew that sometimes a bull wouldn't charge if you moved real slow, but I also knew that those two bulls were getting ready to charge and so did Ed. Ed opened the gate, dashed in, grabbed Fred around the waist, and spun around to exit out the gate.

The bigger of the two bulls let out a deep, rumbling bellow and charged. Ed had broken all records getting out of the gate and slamming it shut, so the bull just skidded up against the gate and fell to one knee. I figured Fred finally knew why he shouldn't be in the pen. I saw Ed shake a bit, and he was madder than a billy goat caught in a barbwire fence.

Just a year ago, Ed had been in an argument with a bull named Blackie, and he almost got whipped good. Ed didn't set Fred down; he just carried him up to the house and told him to stay there until his dad came to get him. Ed later told me the bull would have killed the kid, and nothing could have stopped him.

Ed later told me he was fed up with all of the baloney of having all those town idiots come out to our farm. It caused nothing but trouble and extra work, and if anymore came, he was going to town and stay until fall.

City folks thought our farm was a summer resort...

Later that summer, we had a kid as a guest that was on probation for drunken driving. He was a real loser, and I was glad to see him go. He raised all sorts of havoc: breaking eggs, throwing rocks at the bulls, and swearing all the time. A lot of friends of my folks seemed to think our farm was a summer resort and they should to be treated like royalty.

We had one young lady that Mother showed how to crochet and how to cook a few good meals. She was a pretty, petite girl who never said much, but smiled a lot, and I thought she was a living doll.

She didn't like cows, and when I tried to show her how to milk one, the cow kicked the milk bucket over and did the unmentionable job, which was a real mess. I never saw her after that...

My mother told me that, although she didn't want to wish her life away, she was glad when September rolled around. I was tickled to start back to the country school with the rest of the farm kids.

It was hard to believe that anyone couldn't tell a bull from a cow or a horse from a chicken, and I guessed I was lucky to have been born on a farm. It seemed like I was growing up too fast, but I still liked to catch frogs and tease girls, especially the older ones—just one more benefit of growing up on our farm.

1943

Cleanin' the Barn

I was born on a blackland farm,
Raising hay and planting corn,

Milking cows and pitchin' hay,
And fixin' fence for a twelve-hour day.

Lots of chores that were never done,
Feedin' pigs and heavin' dung,

But of all the chores on our farm,
I hated most cleanin' the barn.

Now I didn't mind feedin' cows the hay,
But cleaning it out ruined my day,

My brother would milk with a gallon pail,
Dodgin' the slaps of a swinging tail,

Laughing as he finished the final cow,
Yelling to me, "It's your turn now."

And the only way I could get my job done
Was pretend that I was having fun.

So I'd grab a fork and a water pail
And stare with hate at the swinging tails,

While my brother said with a wide-toothed grin,
 "It ain't bad, once you begin."

So I'd start the chore with a solemn vow
That I'd never, ever own a cow,

And use no milk 'til my dying day,
Or visit a place that even raised hay.

1952

120

Jack the Mule

What name could be more fitting for a jackass than the name Jack? When I was a young farmer-to-be in 1942, my father brought home to our farm a funny-looking horse. At least, I thought it was a horse because I had never seen a mule. The thing looked like a horse, almost; he was slim-hipped and long-legged with a kind of yellowish hair around his eyes, and his ears were too long, like a jackrabbit's ears. Dad told me that it was a mule and could outwork most horses. He had bought the mule from one of his railroad buddies, who had lost the mule's mate the year before. He had drowned during the spring runoff trying to cross the river on soft ice.

Jack was an ornery old cuss...

We unloaded Jack and led him into the barn to stay for a day or two to get used to it and the stock we kept around it. A couple of days later, we turned him out into the pasture with a retired horse named Kate. The first thing the mule did was to walk by Kate, turn on his front legs, and kick her square in the side with both feet. Kate grunted, fell to her knees, and then slowly got to her feet. She shook her head two or three times, pointed her ears at the mule, and then walked away and stood by the gate like she wanted out.

Old Kate was about 14 years old and gentle as a lamb. She was about 15 hands high and getting a little grey on the muzzle. She had never been rode, was still in excellent shape, and acted more like a colt than an old horse. For the next several days, Kate walked a wide berth around Jack. Whenever Jack would try to get close to Kate, she would lay her ears back and move away. This went on for several days until one afternoon when I was helping put oats in their feeder boxes.

Katie was waiting patiently for supper when the mule ambled up beside her and stood there for a few moments. I thought that they would finally become friends, and I put quite a good helping of oats in the boxes. When I was finished filling the boxes, I stepped back at same time the mule reached over and sank his teeth into Kate's neck. Now, that wasn't a love nibble—like horses do to each other. The darn mule opened his mouth and sank his big, buck teeth into Kate's neck right behind her ears. Kate reared up and so did the mule, but he didn't let go. I've heard horses scream, squeal, and grunt before, but nothing like the sound that came out of Kate's mouth. She whirled around, and pulling loose from the mule, she kicked him in the side with one hind foot. The mule staggered, then turned and ran across the pen, and stood looking at Kate, like he didn't believe what had happened. After that Jack steered clear of Kate and even drank on the opposite side of the water tank. I think he'd figured out that he wasn't the only animal who called the place home.

Jack was also stubborn as —you guessed it—a mule...

We didn't have another mule to work with Jack, and we couldn't hook him up with one of the horses. We tried, but Jack wouldn't budge once he was hitched to anything. He even jumped over the tongue of the rake once, but he wouldn't go forward. So, after several tries, my dad hired Carl, a rancher that lived a few miles away, to bring one of his mules to team up with Jack. He was to rake a 13-acre field with a dump rake and get Jack used to working. What followed was like a circus with untrained animals.

I sat on the fence and watched as Carl led his mule out of his truck to hook it up to the dump rake. Everything went fine. He tied his mule to a post and went to get Jack from the barn. The first thing I heard from the barn was a loud thud, and Carl came sailing out of the barn.

Carl picked himself up and looked at me. He shook his head and said, "That dirty s.o.b. kicked me as I tried to untie him from the stall. Is he always that skittish?" I never answered, and Carl brushed himself off and went back into the barn, closing the bottom half of the door. Our barn doors were divided in half, and the bottom could be closed with the top left open.

A few minutes later, Carl came out of the barn holding his arm. He hollered, "Hey kid, that g.d. mule bit my shoulder, and I can't untie him. Can you bring him out of the barn?"

I climbed down from the fence and went into the barn, walked up to the front of the stall, untied Jack, brought him out, and handed the lead rope to Carl. Carl led Jack over to the dump rake beside his mule and pushed him over the rake tongue to give him room to throw the harness on. Jack laid his ears back, reached over, and bit Carl's mule on the mane right behind the ears. He also tried to kick Carl's mule but instead kicked the tongue of the rake. Carl's mule lunged backward, breaking the tie rope loose from the post.

Then he took off and fleet-footed it down the fence line, dragging the rake and Jack along with him. Carl's mule was pretty strong and, at a half trot, ran the left rake wheel into one of the posts, pushing Jack into the fence. It was lucky that the fence was a jack fence,[4] and the mule wasn't hurt. As the rake came to a sudden halt, the tongue snapped off the rake, and Jack the mule split. Carl's mule stood there, not moving.

Just shoot the s.o.b. and leave him for the coyotes...

We had a devil of a time rounding up Jack. We finally cornered him and led him back to the barn. Carl unhitched his mule from the rake, gathered up his extra harness, and started for the truck. He said there wasn't any way that he would go near Jack or any machinery that Jack was hooked to. I asked him what I should tell my dad, and he said, "Shoot the s.o.b., and leave him for the coyotes."

When Dad came home, he hired a friend to haul Jack to the auction yard. Jack's reputation preceded him, and Dad sold Jack for just $50. All Dad said was, "Heaven help the poor soul that bought that crazy mule." I agreed.

1942

---

[4] Jack fences were built of wood poles on jacks—something like saw horses sitting on top of the ground.

Scratching Out a Living

Farm and ranch life during the late 1930s was tough on everybody: the farmers who grew crops such as corn, oats, and soybeans; and the ranchers who bred and broke good horses to sell. Commodities—as they were called—were still low from the Depression, so there was very little profit in raising anything. Horse ranchers had almost no market for their stock, and in any case, that occupation was slowly disappearing, replaced by cattle and/or sheep. Some tried to raise pigs, cows for milking, or chickens by the hundreds. Some even raised turkeys, ducks, and geese for their feathers and eggs during those hard times.

Families began to slowly disintegrate...

Sundays became just another day: repairing equipment, fixing fence, and checking stock along with a myriad of other chores, most of them done from the back of a horse. Also during time period, families began to slowly disintegrate, some members leaving farms and ranches to find work or to better themselves—never to return.

One of our neighbors just plain gave up, loaded the Model A with odds and ends, locked up the house, and took off for California to try and start over. I had a strong affection for his daughter, and we used to ride some together on their ranch. I'm not too sure whether it was the little Pinto horse she rode or her blonde hair and blue eyes I missed most, but I can vouch for all those kids my age with their terrible lonesome feelings when someone moves away and you know it's for keeps. They called it "puppy love," but it was really hurtful, almost like being smacked in the stomach for no reason.

Even doctors and preachers were scratching for a living...

Necessary services like doctoring and religion became mobile, in that preachers and doctors made regular rounds of the farms in our area—visitations—as they were called, not only to keep their patients in good health both physical and mental, but also to keep reminding them that better times were on the way. In addition to those two objectives, there was also the desire for remuneration to increase their income. The only drawback to this was, most times, the bill was paid in-kind: vegetables, milk, chickens, eggs, and other items were payments of the day. The doctor preferred money, while the minister was happy with anything.

Our preacher spent most of his time talking with the wives, so he never seemed to notice I was even around. I thought he was just a beggar, expecting food from everyone. He had a small son who usually came with him and waited in the wagon. He never failed to stick his tongue out at me as they drove off, and I made a vow to someday give him a black eye.

Hard times—but we made it through...

Not everyone had an automobile in those days, and horse and buggy proved to be the major means of getting about. Visitors would drive their buggy into the yard and tie the reins to a post or tree. The horse would wait, dozing, until time to leave. Some of the buggy riders carried a big round weight with a ring attached to it in their buggy. They would tie the reins to the weight and place it on the ground, and the horse wouldn't move. My dad told me that the weight started the term "ground-tied." Also, there were plenty of saddle horses carrying men up and down the country roads every day. Those were hard times—but we made it through.

1944

Final Ride Home

In April of 1938, a man came riding down our muddy road and up to our house. It was raining and had been miserable all that week. The rider had on a green raincoat that covered him past his knees. His horse was miserably soaked, and the rider's hat was pouring the rain onto the horse's neck in a steady stream. I was standing inside the porch, and I watched as the rider sat still, looking around the yard. Then holding the left rein in his hand, he dismounted and almost fell. He caught his balance and tied his horse to a post we had by the porch. When he saw me, he patted the horse's neck and came up the stairs to the screen door.

He wanted to see his family one last time...

He looked at me for a few seconds and then spoke through the screen door, saying, "Hello there, young fella, do you suppose I could talk to your pa for a minute?"

I told him Dad was not home and called for Mom to come to the door. She came to the front porch, looked at the cowboy, and said, "Oh my God! Samuel, come in, come in."

I opened the door, and he entered, standing on a rug while he removed his hat and raincoat. He followed Mom into the house and sat down at the kitchen table. Mom poured him some coffee, and they talked while I went to feed the cows. When I returned, the man named Sam was gone down to our little bunkhouse, and his horse was still tied to the post. I was told to take the horse to the barn, unsaddle him, and rub him down as best as I could. Mom said that Sam was sick and that she was putting him up until Dad came home. I took the horse out to the barn, unsaddled him, gave him a real big helping of oats, and cleaned him up. The next morning Dad came home, and when I came downstairs, Mom, Dad, and Sam were sitting in the kitchen having coffee and visiting.

Sam knew just about everything that happened in the West...

I sat in the living room and listened to as much of the conversation as I could. Mom had told me that Sam's last name was Coets and that he had spent most of his life from the age of 16 working on ranches in Wyoming and Montana. He had just turned 63 and had returned to his old homestead to see if any of his family was still there. When he couldn't find anyone he knew, he asked the sheriff, and that was how he found our farm.

He talked about his last job—working cows in Montana around the "breaks" in the Missouri River area. He had seen and met some wanted men who worked for different spreads along the river. He had helped push cows into a place named Fort Keogh for the government and for the Indians there. He talked about a fight between Indians and the Army up along the Canadian border quite a few years ago, and he said the Indians finally gave up. He also talked to a couple of riders who had been told of a big fight at a place called Wounded Knee where some Indians had been killed. He said that Montana was pretty well filled up now, and that the Indians mostly stayed in places given to them to live on. He had never married because he never had a chance. He did have a lady friend once in Fort Keogh, but she seemed to have a whole passel of men friends, and she wasn't up to marrying. Sam coughed a lot, looked rather pale, and seemed to have trouble breathing.

Later that day I asked him if he had ever shot anyone. He told me that he had an old pistol, and he showed it to me. It had the initials BRC carved on the grip, and since his name was Sam Coets, I figured he had bought it in Montana. He said he used the gun to kill snakes, and he had a Winchester rifle he used to shoot coyotes and wolves with, which he had sold in South Dakota because he needed the money. He had ridden horseback for over a week to get to our farm, and his horse, Jeb, was plumb wore out and old. Sam never did answer my question; he did say that he was 63 long, hard years young.

Gettin' ready to cash in…

Sam stayed with us for about two months, loafing around and spending time with Dad and in the barn talking to his horse. One night after chores, he had me go to the bunkhouse with him, and he gave me the old pistol, telling me to never shoot it at anything but varmints. I showed it to Dad, and all he said was he would keep it until later. Early one Saturday in June, Mom called me downstairs and asked me to take Sam's horse out to the pasture and to leave the halter on. Then she told me to *not* go near the bunkhouse. I stayed clear of the cabin, but I kept a good eye on it all day long. That afternoon a big black car pulled into the yard and backed up to the cabin. Two men got out of the car, opened the back door of the car, and then entered the cabin carrying a sort of bed. They came right back out with the bed with something that looked like a body on it. They carried it out to the car and put it into the back, slamming the door shut. Then they got back into the car and drove away.

I waited until they were out of sight and entered the cabin. Sam was gone, and so were his clothes, boots, and hat. I had a horrible feeling in my stomach and ran to the house to tell Mom what I had seen. She had me sit down and then told me that Sam had something called Tuberculosis of the lungs. Sleeping on the ground, eating bad food, and smoking and chewing had finally wore out his body. He came to our farm to see his last remaining relative one more time. His only brother had been killed in a car accident and my dad was his second cousin and the only relative he had left. He had been getting sicker and sicker and figured to "cross over" soon. He had wanted to attend church services the previous Sunday, but had been too ill to go.

Sam hung up his spurs...

Our mobile preacher came by the next day and spent most of the day with my folks. They made arrangements for Sam's last rites and planned to have him buried in a small cemetery near our farm, since there were no other relatives. The next afternoon, the big black hearse came into our yard and parked under our big oak tree. The preacher climbed out carrying a Bible, and the driver opened up the back door and the casket so we could see Sam one last time. Then the driver closed the lid of the casket, and the preacher began to speak:

We are here to lay Sam Coets to rest and honor him as a good man. Sam was one of the remaining real-life cowboys who rode the range, doing good as he could, and never asking anyone for help. He climbed down from the saddle for the last time with the realization he was headed for home. He lived a hard life, most of it on the back of a horse, and now he has hung up his spurs. Ashes to ashes and dust to dust is a fitting and proper ending for Sam Coets. Amen.

Mom and Dad were both shedding tears, and I joined in. With that, the hearse drove out of the yard, and the preacher lifted his hand in farewell. Old Sam was gone. One more experience to add to my memories of life and another picture in my mind forever.

1944

Part II

Adventures in Montana

1944 – 1953

Baking Powder Biscuits

From 1943 through 1946, my brother, Tom Anderson, worked on the Newton spread about one mile east of Roundup, Montana, and the Musselshell River. J.W. Newton owned the ranch, and Park Newton, his son, was the ranch manager. J.W. was one of the original entrepreneurs in the Roundup area and knew almost everyone in the area. He rode a horse everywhere he went and smoked long black cigars—he called cigarettes "pimp sticks"—almost to the day he traveled on into the area history books.

Tom spent many evening hours on the ranch visiting with J.W. and Park about the early days as a rancher in the Roundup and Big Wall area. Tom also met quite a bunch of cowhands and area ranchers and accumulated a saddlebag full of stories, both true and fabricated, with a few in between. Some were so bad they seemed to have been scraped off the dirt in the horse corral.

The following story was told to Tom by a local wrangler named Carl in 1946 during branding at the ranch. Carl said the event happened in 1939 out at Big Wall, and he was one of the two riders in the story. Tom re-told the story to me in 1946 and said it was true and accurate as far as he knew. He said that Park Newton and J.W. both stated that Carl was one true cowpoke and had never told a tall tale as far as they knew. The only bad habits that Carl had were chasing the ladies and drinking a snort or two of their moonshine. Other than that, Carl washed regular in the Musselshell and combed his hair about once a week.

Carl told Tom that he and a drifter named Harry worked on ranches all across the Bull Mountain[5] area down along the Musselshell River below Melstone.

---

[5] The Bull Mountains were so named for a giant buffalo bull that ran there and *not* for the stories that came out of the area!

Back in the days when the latchstring was always out...

One spring day, Carl and Harry were offered a job putting up loose hay on a ranch north of Big Wall by a ranch foreman who was short of good hands. The next morning, Carl and Harry saddled up after breakfast, climbed aboard their saddles, and headed north to the Big Wall country on Big Wall Creek. The Big Wall was a sandstone formation 200 feet high that had been thrust up during some pre-historic time and ran unbroken for a mile or so towards the east. A rancher named Jerry and his wife Lilly had ranched in that area for quite a few years and were well-known for their hospitality and the Herefords they raised. Their ranch was about half way to the ranch that Carl and Harry were headed for, so when they got to Jerry's ranch, they decided to hang up their spurs until the next morning. They threw their broncs into the small corral, hung their saddles on the wood fence rail, fed their horses some hay and oats, and went up to the ranch house to find something to eat. In the late 1930s, it was still okay to enter a ranch house if no one was home and the door was unlocked. It was also okay to fix up a meal as long as you cleaned up your mess and left the kitchen as you found it. There was a note on the front door that said, "Welcome to our ranch, make yourself at home."

They were cowboys, not cooks...

Carl said that they were hungry enough to eat an uncooked possum except for the claws, so they decided to cook something up to tide them over until they got to their new job.

They found some limp vegetables on the back porch and a chunk of cured ham that wasn't all green, so they fired up the wooden cook stove, put a big pan full of water on the top, threw all of the vegetables and the whole chunk of ham into the pot, and sat down at the table to wait for supper. Harry remarked to Carl that some biscuits would be mighty tasty and volunteered to make a batch. He found some hog lard, salt, and a bag of flour—but no baking powder. Carl had been looking in the coat closet, and he yelled to Harry that he had found a can of Calumet baking powder on the top shelf, pushed up against the wall. He threw it to Harry, who noticed the lid was taped down; written on the side of the can was "Rose - 1939." Harry figured that was the date it was bought, so he cut the tape to open the can.

He dumped out a handful and said, "Hey Carl, this stuff is grey instead of white, so it must be pretty old."

Carl hollered back, "It don't hurt bakin' powder to be old. Don't worry. Go ahead and use it."

Harry mixed up all of the needed ingredients in a bowl, added water, and then rolled the dough out on the table with a fruit jar. He used a jar lid to cut out the biscuits, put them on a tray in the oven, and shut the oven door. Carl had the table all set, and in a few minutes, Harry removed the pan of biscuits from the oven and dumped them on the table. When they hit the table, they sounded like a batch of horseshoes dumped on the table. The two famished cowhands sat down at the table, and Carl said, "Them are the dumbest biscuits I've ever seen. They're flatter than a frozen cow pie in December and harder than a frozen horse turd. But we can dunk them into the coffee, and they'll probably be okay." The two ate everything on the table, cleaned up their mess, and bedded down in the barn. Come sun up, they were on their way north before breakfast to start their new job.

The summer rushed by, and when haying was done, the two hands headed south, only to stop at Jerry's ranch to rest and feed their horses. This time, the folks were home. Harry and Carl had done a little fishing in Big Wall Creek and caught a few brook trout, which they handed to Lilly to cook up for supper. Soon there was a fish dinner on the table, and they all sat down to eat. Carl began to eat and mentioned to Lilly about their other stay at the ranch and all about the rock-hard biscuits they had made with the outdated baking powder. Lilly stopped eating and remarked, "I've never used baking powder for baking. I only use yeast to bake with. You must be mistaken."

Carl stopped eating and said, "We found the old can of baking powder in the coat closet and used some of it to raise the biscuits. It must have been defective because it was grey and didn't help the biscuits at all."

You two idiots ate my mother...

Lilly never said a word; she just pushed back her chair, rose from the table, and walked to the coat closet. She rummaged around, and sure enough, she found the Calumet baking powder can. The can felt awfully light, and she removed the lid, looking into an almost empty can. Lilly came back to the table, sat down, and looking at Carl, said, "We had my mother staying with us these past several years. When she passed away last year, we had her cremated in Billings, Montana. We didn't have an urn for her ashes, so the undertaker gave us this Calumet can. Didn't you two see her name and the date on the side of the can?" She sat there for a few minutes and then remarked, "You two idiots ate my mother."

Carl said that he and Harry went out, saddled up, and hastily left. He said that Harry rode straight west, and he returned to Roundup. He also said that he could never eat another bakin' powder biscuit.

1946

Big Elk Prospector

I was visiting my brother Tom one Sunday on Tilford "Til" Sedgwick's S Lazy T spread on the Big Elk River to do some fishing and relaxing. It was in July of 1948, and the weather was perfect for enjoying the river. When we returned to the house, I made the comment that the "dad-blamed" river was colder than an ice cube in December. Til said that the start of the Big Elk River was a huge, fat snow bank, and the river stayed cold all the way to Lebo Lake. I asked him if anyone had ever found gold at the head of the river, and he told me that a few men had been up and down the river over the years, but he thought that they were all nuts. He said the Crazy Mountains seemed to attract crazies from all over. He said he didn't know of any gold found and he didn't think anyone was up there this year. I told Tom we should take a trip up there and see if anything was happening on the river. Til said to go ahead, but watch out for all the buffalo because the one thing they didn't like was "uppity school kids."

L to R: Al Anderson, Donna Sedgwick, and Tom Anderson.
S Lazy T Ranch, Two Dot, Montana. 1947.

Hold it right there—you're trespassing on my claim...

The next Sunday, my brother Tom picked me up in Til's pickup, and we headed up the valley towards the foothills of the Crazies. On the way up the valley, Tom stopped at an old buffalo jump where we found some stone arrowheads. We drove up the valley as far as we could and then walked for what seemed like miles. We finally saw an old—used to be white—tent on the south side of the Big Elk. It was worn, tattered and torn, and looked uninhabited. We walked a little closer and could see a couple pairs of socks and a pair of pants hanging on a rope, tied between two trees. I told Tom that someone was in the tent, and whoever it was hadn't heard us because of the roaring noise the river was making. As we got closer, we could smell the aroma of boiling coffee, and we expected to see a huge dog guarding the tent, but didn't see one. There was a mule staked out in a small clearing beyond the tent.

Tom and I were standing still about 60 feet from the tent when we heard someone yell, "Hold it right there. You're trespassing on my claim." A man walked out of the tent holding a double-barreled shotgun pointed at the sky, and we heard the click as he cocked one

135

barrel of the gun. He stood there with two rubber boots in his other hand and a beat-up old felt hat on his head. He was about six feet tall and skinny as a chicken with a broken beak. "What do you guys want?" he asked, making no move to lower the gun. "How many more of your friends are out there?"

Tom and I were the only ones there except a few fat steers and maybe a deer or two. I told him that we were working for John Miller on the Top Hat Ranch, and that we just wanted to see what was at the head of the Big Elk River.

He slowly lowered the shotgun and said, "Come on up and sit a spell." We did just that and sat discussing the Top Hat and John Miller and Alvin Berg. His name was Frank, and he was originally from Helena, Montana. He said he knew Miller and had seen him a few times in the past year or so. He told us he had been prospecting for gold around there for the past three years. He had found a tiny amount, but not enough to sell. We asked him why he didn't get a dog to watch his camp and warn trespassers away. He said he used to have a collie named Felix, but he had died a week or so ago. He offered us some of his coffee, but we declined and hung around for about two hours just talking. I felt sorry for the prospector, who looked tired, hungry, and alone.

Pretty dang lonesome up in the mountains...

During our conversation, Frank mentioned that he had been shot at a few times by hunters, and that a couple of them gave him a hard time last fall. He said he usually left the camp in October to winter in Harlowton or Lewistown. Every spring for the past three years, when he returned to his camp, he found the tent ropes cut into pieces and all of his gear scattered around the campsite. Frank had a pretty good idea who was doing it, and he said if the s.o.b. ever came around, he could give him a good reason to stay away for the rest of his life. His "good reason" would be a load of buckshot to speed the s.o.b. down the mountain.

Tom and I had spent almost the whole day on this trip, and when we left, Frank said, if we came back, to bring him some coffee, sugar, salt, and tobacco; Tom and I figured that that miner was as lonesome as a prairie dog without a burrow. It was about two weeks later that Tom came by the Top Hat on a Sunday in Til's old pickup. Sitting in the seat with Tom was a big brown and white dog that Tom called Junior. He had picked the dog up from the vet in Harlo and was taking the dog and a few things up to the miner. He wanted me to go along, but we had been working seven days a week to finish putting up hay at the Top Hat, and I couldn't take time off. I told Tom to call out the miner's name real loud for the last 100 feet or so to let him know he was coming.

Tom told me, when he returned from the trip, that he gave Frank all of the supplies he had asked for and included a box of candy bars and a sack of dog food for the new dog. When he started to leave the prospector to return down the mountain, the prospector had some grit in his eyes that made them water real bad.

Tom and I never saw Frank again. One Saturday in September on his way to buy some supplies at the Two Dot Merc, Frank asked Til Sedgwick if Tom was still working there. When Til told him that Tom and his brother had returned to Roundup to go to school, the prospector said, "Those are a couple of real good men." Til told Tom about the comment the following summer. Mining gold in the Crazy Mountains was lonesome work.

1950

Big Red

In the fall of 1945, I became acquainted with a cutting horse named Big Red—15 hands high and a head full of savvy. He was owned by a horseman named Elmer Hinton, who raised horses on a small spread north of Roundup out in the Big Wall country. Elmer had trained Red well. When you wanted to cut any cow out of a herd, all you had to do was start the process, and Red did the rest of the work. Once the chosen victim was prodded to move, Red stayed right on it, moving from side to side, leaving no room or opportunity for the animal to veer away. Besides his ability to work cows, Red was gentle and not a bit skittish.

He just didn't want anyone to boss him around…

Elmer raised horses, a few cows, chickens, sage hens, and a few prairie dogs. His ranch raised more sagebrush than hay so Elmer cut everything he could. He had an alfalfa field and some oats, and he kept the small willows cut down to mix them with the hay for feed. He was a bachelor by choice, and he told me he had never married because he had never found anyone he liked well enough to want to give up the way of living he dearly loved—and he didn't want someone to boss him around. He figured that he and Red could get along just fine with a bit of grub and a pitchfork full of hay. He said it was great to be able to get up in the morning, throw a handful of coffee grounds into the old pot, and not catch hell for not washing three times a day. I totally agreed with that idea because I didn't think water should be wasted just to wash hands.

I spent over a month with Elmer, and he did all of the cooking, although he did allow me to make coffee a couple of times. Every meal we ate during that time consisted of coffee, bread, a piece of antelope meat, and a whole bunch of potatoes covered with gravy. Whenever we had a visitor or two that stayed for breakfast, we had dollar-sized pancakes, a bowl full of scrambled eggs, cured ham slices, and coffee. He was a loner and loved to read by lamp light, sometimes into the early morning hours. He also smoked Bull Durham cigarettes, but he never chewed tobacco.

Every morning, Elmer would go out to the barn to let Big Red out of his stall to eat, drink, and get exercise. Elmer really loved that big red horse, and the horse reciprocated, following Elmer around all he could. There was an incentive to that— Elmer carried some sugar cubes in his pocket and gave Red one or two every day. Elmer had a few head of Herefords that he raised for cash, and he kept Red in shape by rounding them up from time to time and moving them around the pasture. He always cut out one of them and let Red take the animal right into the corral. Then Elmer would turn the cow loose to join the rest of the herd.

There were quite a few coyotes on the Big Wall, and Elmer told me that, when the coyotes on the Big Wall hollered, cried, and yelped at night, it was like a good chorus of lovesick dogs that reminded him of the lonesome nights on the prairie in the late 1920s. He said it was a call for companionship and anticipation of finding a sweetheart. I personally thought that it was a terribly lonely cry, more like mourning than elation. A year or two before, someone had shot a coyote mother. Elmer found two pups hungry and crying. He brought them to his cabin, fed them for a few days, and then turned them loose. They ran off, but later returned to sit by the barn and cry with little yelping sounds, like they wanted some more of his cooking. When they finally ran off, they didn't return, and he missed them. He said that Red never did take to them and, whenever he saw them, he would snort and paw the dirt.

Just helping his neighbor out by keeping his milk cow...

Elmer always saddled Red and rode around his spread, checking fences and looking for stray cows and horses that sometimes got into his hayfield. He told me that he once discovered a dairy cow in his alfalfa field. He had brought her into the barn where he kept her for a few days until he found out where she belonged. He said she hadn't been milked for a while and was dripping milk as she walked. He said, "I brought her home, threw her into the barn, and helped out the dairy by milking her for a few days. I gave the milk to my chickens, at least what I had left, after I drank some." Then he grinned and walked towards the barn.

As we walked to the barn, he told me that some hired man in a pickup came to take her home. When he tried to get her into the truck, she charged him and tried to butt him with her hornless head. Elmer said that maybe she liked him and wanted to stay where she was, but they finally got her into the truck and took off for home.

I helped Elmer take out a busted-up cattle guard, and we laid it inside the gate so the welder could get to it. We figured the welder would spot it and weld it back together so we could re-install it. The next morning the welder drove his pickup up to the gate, unlatched it, and then drove his truck right into the hole. He buried his truck up to the frame; the front tires were hidden, and the tailgate stuck up into the air. He climbed out of the truck, spit out a few choice adjectives, and came walking towards the house. Elmer headed to the barn to harness the team of horses to—as Elmer put it—"pull the dummy out." After we got the truck out of the hole, the welder told Elmer that we should have left the guard outside the gate where he could see it. Elmer was a quiet man and never wasted words. After he paid the welder and thanked him, Elmer said, "I'd hate to ride too far with that guy. He sure doesn't have any sense; even old Red wouldn't have walked into that ditch."

Old Red was put down in 1951 and was buried out by the Big Wall where he loved to run.

1951

Bill and the '37 Chevrolet

One Saturday morning in September of 1945, I was invited by a couple of ranchers I knew—Bill Kombol and Junior Mikkelson—to ride along with them to the Elliot Sheep Ranch up north of Lavina, Montana. At that time, I was working at Kibble & Case Cigar Store in Roundup, Montana, and I had the weekend off. I thought that the trip would be a relaxing, one-day jaunt. We would run up Saturday morning and return that night after dark. I knew the Elliot family, and their son Bob was a good rancher and a good cook. I was looking forward to eating a home-cooked meal and the chance to see Bob. The only comment I had gotten about the trip was from Albert Greener, a good friend who told me that the weather might turn overnight. He also told me that all of the buffalo on the way up there might stampede and cause a riot. Junior Mikkelson was about my age, and his family ranched down east of town. He was a real quiet man and totally afraid of anything that had more than two legs because he had been attacked by a range bull a few years back, and it had stomped him pretty good.

Just a relaxing jaunt for the day...
Junior and I were good friends, and he came into Kibble & Case often to visit. We had discussed the trip and thought it would

140

be fun. We decided to leave our coats at home because we would be coming right back. Besides, it was Indian Summer and about 70 degrees during the day. I threw several candy bars in a sack and filled up Junior's canteen for the next morning. Bill Kombol met us at Kibble's the next morning at 7:00 a.m., and we climbed into a 1937 Chevrolet that belonged to Bill's brother Joe. I looked at Junior and whispered that 1937 Chevys were known for clutches that slipped, and that I hoped we'd make it up to Elliot's and back okay. It had rained some, and the famous farm roads would be as slick as a greased pig.

For those not familiar with the term "gumbo," it is a word used by ranchers to describe the top layer of most of the roads in the eastern part of Montana. It stood for thick, slick, and sticky, and no one was able to navigate on it after a rainstorm. If the top two inches of the road received moisture, the road became slicker than Vaseline on a doorknob.

I had first-hand knowledge of being stranded in a bed of gumbo out on Elmer Hinton's spread. I had ridden in a horse-drawn hayrack in October of 1943 out in the Big Wall country. I was helping Elmer get a load of hay to put into his barn, and a rainsquall had wet down the trail we were using. We were ready to go when the short rainstorm hit. When it finally quit raining, we waited about an hour and then headed out to get the hay from a stack in the field. We made the trip out and loaded the hay as it began to sprinkle again. As we started back to the barn, we made it about 500 feet before the wheels had built up to twice their size and the horses couldn't move the hayrack. It took us a couple of hours to pry the gumbo off the wheels and from the undercarriage. When we finally arrived at the barn, the hayrack was carrying about 200 pounds of gumbo.

So when it began to lightly rain on the asphalt road to Lavina, it posed no problem. I told Junior that, if the rain continued on the road to the sheep ranch, we might have a hard time making the trip. It rained all the way to the Lavina turnoff. When Bill pulled the car onto the dirt road that would take us to Elliot's, the car almost slid off the road because it was so slick. Bill straightened out the car, and since the drive wheels spun a lot on the clay road, he had to slip the clutch to keep the car on the road. If he hadn't slipped the clutch, we would have slid off the road and sunk up to the frame in the mud and water-filled ditch. It seemed like all the animals along the road—deer, calves, and cows—stopped eating to stare at us, just like we were stupid…

I bet you're glad we don't raise elephants…

We finally drove into Elliot's ranch after stopping twice to dig the brown mud out of the wheel wells of the big car. Bill had slipped the clutch so much that the car would barely move, and the motor was racing like we were doing 75 miles an hour. We spent the rest of the day sitting in the kitchen of the ranch house, visiting with Bob. About 7:00 p.m., Bob made a small supper that was downright tasty. We had to sleep over because we had wasted the whole day just getting there. It rained all the time we were there, and Bill spent the next day moving sheep. We tried to get Bob to drive us to Lavina so we could catch a ride home, but he said, "Not in this mess."

Finally, about 4:00 p.m., Bill came riding back to the corral, unsaddled, turned the horse loose, and came to the house. He was a muddy, gosh-awful mess, looking like a survivor from a tornado. His coat was torn, his Levis were torn down one leg, and his boots were two big balls of mud. He never did explain what exactly had transpired, but it looked like every animal in the area had deliberately walked all over him. All he said was that he had got into a bunch of sheep, slipped off his horse, and had to crawl out on his hands and knees. He said that one of the rams attacked him, and he had a devil of a time convincing the ram that he was not one of the woolies. All Bob Elliot said was, "By hell, Bill, I bet that you're glad we aren't raising elephants!"

It was growing dark when the three of us climbed into Bill's borrowed car and started up the hill. The county road was about 50 feet higher than the ranch house, and though it had stopped raining, the farm road was so slick we could not make it up the hill. So Bill drove in a big circle, sped up, and tried to climb the hill again. Halfway up, the car came to a halt and wouldn't budge. After a few minutes of waiting, we tried again. The car moved about two feet, slid back about five feet, and came to a solid halt. The wheels were plugged up, and the clutch couldn't force the wheels to turn.

I looked at Bill and told him the clutch plate must be burned out, probably from slipping it on the way up. He agreed, got out, and opened the trunk to get a few tools. He crawled under the car, and using a flashlight to find the clutch-adjusting rod, he took up all the slack he could. He yelled for help, and Junior and I pulled him out from under the car. He was covered with mud, so he took off his cap, coat, shoes, and pants and threw them into the trunk. He looked so funny with just long underwear and socks on that we all had a big laugh. When we started the car, it climbed the hill, and we were on the way home.

Tell me again why you're driving in your long johns...

The road from Lavina to Roundup is a narrow, two-lane, blacktopped highway. The speed limit was 35 mph, and Bill was running about 50. We were on the long hill coming down to Elso Dairy, just west of Elso, when Bill said, "Sh**," and pulled the car over to the side of the road. I looked out the back window and could see a highway patrol car with lights flashing coming to a stop behind us. The only other thing on the highway was a deer, so I knew we had been speeding and had got caught.

The patrolman climbed out of his car and walked up to talk with Bill. It had to be about speeding. His Levis were in the trunk as was his wallet, and Bill said, "Damn," under his breath.

The patrolman was cheerful as he asked Bill for his driver's license. The metal nameplate on his shirt read, "Max Blakley." Bill looked up at the patrolman for a few seconds and then said, "I'll have to get it out of the trunk," as he started to push his door open.

The patrolman pushed the door back shut and said, "How come it's in the trunk?" Junior and I never said a word.

Bill scratched his head and said, "It's a long story." Then he told the patrolman that, if he could get out, he'd open up the trunk and dig it out.

The patrolman looked at me and Junior and then said, "You know, you look like something else; underwear and socks aren't exactly dress clothes. If you'll hand me your keys and then tell me your story, we'll see."

Good old Montana gumbo is to blame for everything...

Bill thought a minute and then said, "Rain caused this whole mess, that and these g.d. gumbo roads. My name's William Kombol, and I ranch northwest of Roundup with my two brothers, Frank and Joe. This is Joe's car, and I borrowed it to drive up to the Elliot Sheep Ranch, north of Lavina, to help with several bands of sheep. The two guys in back are friends who rode along." Bill scratched his head and then said, "We didn't have any trouble until the rain started as I pulled into Lavina and headed north. After a mile or two, the road got slick as a greased cow's tail, and we had a tough time going. I had to ride the clutch for several miles, and that must have ruined the clutch because the car didn't go right. The damned tires built up a pretty good coating of gumbo mud, and we had to use a screw driver and a jack handle to clear out the wheel wells.

"That was one hell of a job, but we finally got to Elliot's and let the car rest a day or two. We got all of the sheep taken care of and started back to Roundup." Bill stopped for a second, and then he said, "When we got ready to come back out of Elliot's, the car just wouldn't go. I had to crawl under it to adjust the clutch rod in the rain and mud, and it was one hell of a chore. Those two men in back had to pull me out from under the car—I was so mired down in the mud. Ask those guys in back; they'll tell you. The reason I took my clothes off was they were filthy and would have ruined the seat in my brother's car."

The patrolman looked at me and said, "You work for Kibble & Case, don't you?" I told him I did and vouched for Bill's strange tale. I also told him that Junior was from a ranch east of Roundup. The patrolman digested all of what he had been told, then opened

144

the car door, and told Bill to set right there. Then he went to the back of the car and retrieved Bill's Levis. They must have weighed 50 pounds with all of the mud. Bill reached into his pants, retrieved his wallet, and showed the patrolman his driver's license.

As the patrolman was looking at Bill's license, Bill said, "Do me a favor and throw those jeans back into the trunk."

The patrolman stood there for a few seconds; then, laying the pants on the hood of the car, he said, "That's the darnedest tale I've ever heard. I don't think anyone else would ever believe you, but it looks like you're telling the truth. I'm not going to cite you for speeding, but keep the speedometer on 35 from now on." He touched the bill of his cap and said, "Have a safe trip home." He walked back to his patrol car and waited for Bill to drive off.

After we arrived back in Roundup, Hap Kibble asked me why I hadn't worked, and I told him I just took a couple of days off. Bill told me later that he got the third degree from his brother about his stay of an extra day at Elliot's. He said that, with it being so late, no one would believe his story. He told Joe that he had a little trouble getting all the sheep moved. Then he buried the dirty clothes out on the prairie. He also told Joe that his car ran just great.

Every time I ran into Bill after that, we both had a good laugh. His ending comment was usually, "Why in the devil don't they build houses out of that gumbo mud? The only thing that could destroy them would be another big flood."

1945

Billy Pruitt—Cowboy

In the early 1940s, I worked with a cowhand in the Big Wall country north of Roundup helping a rancher named Elmer Hinton brand a few horses. Elmer raised some of the best horseflesh in the state, and was pretty stove up from working with them over the years. Elmer had forgot more about horses than most people ever knew. When he asked me to give him a hand, I figured to help him out before I was to go to work for the Milwaukee Railroad.

Better to be a has been, than a never was...

Elmer had also hired a grub line rider named Billy Pruitt to help him, and when I met Billy, I could tell that his luck had been mostly bad over the years. His boots were run down and cracked, and his clothes were threadbare and headed for the scrap pile in the near future. His bedroll looked as if he had used it for many years. His Stetson was ringed with sweat, with a small hole in the crease where it had wore through from lots of use. His horse was in good condition, and though his saddle had a few more rivets than originally used, it was well-oiled and rode quiet as a mouse on a new carpet. When I shook his hand, I could tell that he had worked without gloves for a long time—his hand felt like dried leather with calluses. He did not chew or smoke because he said tobacco made him horribly sick.

That first night we talked for about two hours, and he asked me where I was from. When I told him I was recently from Portland, Oregon, where my dad was an engineer. We hit it off right away. He said that he had hopped a lot of boxcars over the years. He said the best rail line to ride was the Milwaukee because the bulls[6] didn't get nasty if they caught you riding free. I guessed him to be about 50, and he said he'd been born in Chicago in 1898. He had run away from an apprentice job to a blacksmith when he was 14 and had lived on a horse ever since. He said he had worked all one summer for his first horse, an old mare that had every ailment in the vet's bible.

She was a pretty, freckled-up little filly...

The next day, I watched him bring in nine head of horses, and he sat his saddle like he had roots in the darned thing. While we were getting to work on the horses, he told me that, a few years before, he had worked on a spread in Texas down along the Pecos River. He said the foreman had a young daughter, and he helped her at her chores whenever he could. She was a pretty, freckled-up little filly, and he got to really like her. Then one day when he was helping her bring in some wood for the stove, she fell and hurt her

---

[6] Railroad police.

ankle. He picked her up to carry her into the house, and about that time, her dad came riding into the yard, saw him holding her, jumped off his horse, and beat the tar out of Billy. He threw Billy off the ranch and wouldn't listen to what had really happened. Billy said that she wasn't the prettiest girl he'd ever seen, but she was well fed, and he enjoyed her laughter and disposition.

He was just out of luck and from another era…

From there Billy had drifted up into Kansas and worked some around that area. Finally, he thought he'd move on up to Montana to where the really big spreads were said to be hiring. He said he came up through Nebraska and didn't find any work there. Those ranches weren't like the big Texas spreads where it took a week to ride around them. All this time, he'd been hard put to find work on any cow spread, and it was almost impossible to ride anywhere because of all the fences and roads, and besides, shotgun pellets stung pretty bad when caught trespassing. I figured that Billy was quickly running out of time to continue his way of life. His idea of being a cowhand, free to wander about at will, was long over. He was already 30 years or more out of that era. One night after a supper of beans, potatoes, bread, and coffee, he told me that, when this job was finished, he was going to go up into Canada—somewhere around Calgary—where there was still open range left. He said he knew the winters were bad, but freezing to death or starving to death have the same ending. Besides, he had heard that the red-coated police never bothered any Americans.

His time of riding the open range was long gone…

Billy told me that he used to have an old dog for company, but he got snake bit and died. He said it got pretty lonesome out on the prairie, especially at night with nobody to talk with. Later on that week on Sunday, he was riding out on the Big Wall area when a big badger spooked his horse. Caught unawares, his horse threw him in a mess of rocks and broke his right arm just below his elbow. Elmer had to take Billy into Roundup to have his arm set and a cast put on. He had a tough time working after that because he was right-handed. Elmer paid him a month's wages, and he rode off north toward the Missouri Breaks.

I never heard about him again, but I assumed he made it up to the land of northern lights. Up until that time, I had never before seen a man who looked so low in spirit as Billy did riding away on his horse, down on his luck, with only a bedroll, a horse, and $10 folding money to see him through to better times.

1948

Billy

For many years, whenever I needed a haircut and a little uplift in spirit, I would patronize the little barbershop across from the Northern Pacific train depot on Montana Avenue. Old Jim, the barber, did a pretty fair job of mowing and always provided a resume' of what had transpired since the last visit, but the real attraction for many of the regulars was a man named Billy. He was a black man in his late 40s and was a dedicated worker. He had an exceptional memory, a quick wit, and a big smile. He could put a polish on shoes that would last almost as long as the shoe. During the many years that I got clipped by that barber, only one incident remains fresh in my memory.

Get a haircut and a shoeshine while you waited for the train...

Back in the good old days, when the Northern Pacific was offering first class transportation to travelers on a regular basis, all trains stopped in Billings to entrain and exit passengers who were continuing further via other modes of transportation. Sometimes the stop would only be a few minutes. At other times, it would be an hour or two, and some of the passengers would detrain for refreshments in the cafe' or merely wander up and down Montana Avenue. At any rate, the barber shop usually crowded in a few rush jobs, some customers returning from time to time or passing the word on to other travelers that expert, fast service from a barber was available adjacent to the depot.

148

One Friday afternoon, I was in the area and stopped in the barbershop for a trim and an hour of relaxation. When I entered the shop, Billy was sweeping up and told me to have a chair. He remarked that Jim was out for a few minutes, but he could shine my shoes if I wanted. I declined and sat in one of the line chairs to wait and to visit with Billy. We just visited about nothing in particular—the nice weather, the fact that someday the city would cover up the cobbles that made up the street, the trains that were running late—just this and that. He finished sweeping and put on a white apron, explaining that his grey aprons were all dirty, and though he hated to dirty up a brand new white one, he didn't want to ruin his clothes. I nodded and picked up a Saturday Evening Post and started to look at the cartoons. I heard a train pull into the depot and looked up to see a man coming over to the shop. He was huge and looked like an ex-fighter. He entered the door and sat down in one of the two barber chairs. Looking at Billy, he said, "Trim it up." He loosened his tie and leaned back with his eyes closed.

Billy looked at me and said, "You'll have to wait, mister."

But the man said, "Dammit, I've only got a few minutes. Hurry up," and settled back down in the chair.

Billy'd seen Old Jim cut hair for ten years, surely Billy could...

Billy had been with the shop for about ten years, and as he told me later, he figured he could just touch the guy's hair up a bit and avoid any trouble, so he stepped in behind the chair and picked up the clippers. I knew it was a mistake, but I also figured it was none of my business, so I just shook my head at Billy and went back to the magazine, watching carefully over the top.

Billy turned the clippers on and then turned them off. He picked up the straight razor and made a few passes at the strop. He turned on the hot water and then turned it off. Finally, I guess he figured he had stalled long enough. He picked up the white cover and carefully placed it over the customer. He wrapped a white towel around the man's neck and snugged up the white cover tight. Then he picked up the clippers and turned on the switch, watching me with big eyes. I ducked behind the magazine and pretended to be fully occupied with reading.

I heard the clippers start to cut and looked up at Billy. He was standing to one side of the back mirror so I could see the back of the man's head. I almost got up and ran. Right up the back of the head in the middle was a bare strip—from the collar to the top. Billy had run the clippers against the man's head instead of on a comb and had really sheared him. Billy looked all shook up. I could see the cuffs of his pants quivering, he was shaking so bad.

For a few seconds, Billy just stood there looking at the swath he had cut. Then the customer said, "Hurry it up or I'll miss my train."

Billy took a deep breath and started in again. I figured Billy was going to try and even it up a little. I stepped to the door to see if there was a policeman about, because I figured that a felony would be committed as soon as Billy was finished. As I stepped out the door, Billy said, "You're next. Don't go. I'll be done here in a minute." I knew he was scared that I would leave him to a horrible fate, so I went back in and sat down.

The only thing Billy didn't do was nick him…

The more Billy clipped, the worse the job looked. I used to see haircuts like that when I was a kid on our farm, but that was when your mother cut your hair with a pair of sewing scissors. The poor guy looked like hell. All the hair was gone from both sides of his head, and it looked like someone had placed a bowl on the top of his head and cut away all the hair not covered. The only thing that Billy didn't do was nick him, so that he slept on, blissfully unaware of what was happening. When Billy had finished with all of the damage that he could possibly do, he picked up the straight razor and started to strop it, looking at me. I shook my head and rolled my eyes up. Billy was shaking so bad I figured that he would cut the man's throat. Billy stood there for a few minutes, trying to decide what to do. Then he suddenly jerked off his apron, tapped the guy on the shoulder, said, "The haircut's free," and ran out the door.

The man in the chair pulled off the apron and nodded to me in an affable way. He turned to the mirror and stood stunned for about ten seconds. Then he let out a roar and spat out a string of oaths including some I had not heard for years. He raced out of the shop in pursuit of Billy, yelling, "I'll kill that little s.o.b.!" He ran down the street, but Billy was gone.

A career change just seemed like a good idea…

I was looking down the street after him when I felt eyes on the back of my head. Turning, I saw Billy standing by the back door, panting and asking if the victim was gone. I nodded, and as I turned back to the street, I heard the train whistle for "all aboard." I watched as the ex-customer, clipped for fair, returned to the depot, watching the barbershop and swearing a blue streak. After the train had pulled out, Billy quit shaking and sat down in the barber chair. He sat there for a few minutes and then said, "You know, Al. I think I'll get into another line of work and get away from this shop."

When Jim finally got back, Billy had gathered up his gear and had gone. I filled Jim in on what had transpired, and he laughed so hard he almost died. I never did get my hair cut that day. Billy took the Greyhound Bus to Miles City, Montana, where he went to work in the hotel as a bellboy and a shoeshine entrepreneur. I saw him once after that horrible experience, and he asked me if the clipped customer ever came back. I told Billy I had never seen him again.

1951

Boots, Broncs, and Bull Riders

The Harlowton, Montana, Rodeo—July 4, 1947, the Greatest Sports Event in the Heart of Wheatland County. The title says it all. Ranch hands, bronc riders, bull riders, and barrel racers, and not to be left out, all the people involved in the production needed to ensure that it would be the greatest show to date. All the events were dangerous, and caution was the order of the day. The clowns, the chute tenders, the stock handlers, the timekeepers, the pickup riders, and the emergency medical staff were all nervously alert and constantly moving about. The audience was not overly conscious of all the people involved; they were too busy having a good time, helped along by the noise, spirits, and excitement in the rodeo grounds.

The biggest inducement was fast money, plain and simple...

From my personal experience around rodeos, visiting with riders and competitors, I deciphered the following from many different people. The biggest inducement for all rodeo competitors was the chance to make money fast. One rider told me that—if you simply ignored the fact that, in order to win, you had to climb onto the back of a mean and hateful horse weighing a half ton or more, that hated anything on his back, and whose sole intention was to eliminate the rider as fast as possible—you might get lucky and stay aboard for eight seconds. The same was true of bulls, except they had one more incentive: after getting rid of the rider, to either stomp him into the dirt or stick a horn through his body and toss him into the air. The fans eagerly look forward to the mayhem when a bull and his tormentor emerge from the chute. From the get-go, the bull is destined to win the contest unless the rider has the right amount of intestinal fortitude to out-guess the crazy mind of the bull and can hang on his slippery hide for eight seconds— actually a lifetime—depending on the bull.

The Top Hat Crew...

The Top Hat crew at that time was Alvin Berg, Ray Lannen, John Drogitis, and me. Alvin was the foreman and the only one with an automobile, so we all rode with him whenever we went to town. Alvin was a hard-working hand and knew almost everyone in Wheatland County. A better person and ranch hand would be very hard to find. Alvin told us that a clown with a trained buffalo would also be there to "fight" the hump-back bulls. Ray Lannen said that this would be the best Saturday we would see.

The first three ranches above Lebo Lake were owned and operated by members of the Martin family: Dana Martin, Tilford

"Til" Sedgwick, and Wayne Martin. Gib McFarland owned the ranch above those three; it was operated by Pete White. The Top Hat was owned by Pete McKay of Roscoe and managed by John Miller. All were excellent ranchers and enjoyed anything to do with rodeoing. They worked hard, and all interacted with each other and all the hands. It was not unlike one devil of a large family with half a hundred relatives and friends occupying the whole area. Most of the crews rode well and could even last a few jumps on a frisky horse. The best bronc rider I ever knew was Ray Lannen, who hailed from Roscoe. He was strong as an ox, and I never heard anyone give him any grief.

Earlier that June, we were throwing a bridge across the Big Elk River when the tractor we were using became high-centered on a

Al Anderson. 1946.

rock in the river. No one could budge it. I watched for a bit and then grabbed up a pry bar, waded out into the river, stuck the pry bar under the front of the tractor, and lifted it off the big flat rock. I took a bit of grief over that, and "Strong Man" became my nickname for the summer. I never had a problem with any other ranch hand after that, and I did enjoy a beer or two—no charge—at the Two Dot Bar.

The whole Top Hat crew got the day off to celebrate the 4th of July, 1947, and we had looked forward to the rodeo all week. Come Saturday, we all put on our cleanest shirts with buttons and no holes, climbed into our best pair of Levis, and spent some time shining our boots on the back of our pant legs. Slicking our hair down so our Stetsons could cover all of it, we all climbed into Alvin's Ford sedan and peeled out for Two Dot to begin the day. On the way we stopped at the S Lazy T Ranch, Til Sedgwick's spread, and gathered up my brother, Tom, so he could enjoy the day with us. We headed for the Two Dot Bar first to visit with Bill Trautman and to hoist a few beers to get us the 20 miles to Harlowton. We discussed the fact that Alice Greenough would be at the rodeo and that alone made it attending, and the bull-riding event was sure to be a treat.

We arrived in Harlowton just about noon. Alvin Berg had his hands full as he tried to keep track of his carload of ranch hands. He finally said, "All right, men. If you don't meet me at the Graves Hotel to go home at 2:00 a.m., I'll swing by the sheriff's office before I leave." We all knew Alvin was serious, and that statement kept us out of too much trouble.

Never upset a railroader unless you're close to a hospital...

We spent the next hour and a half checking out the bars. We imbibed several beers, and everyone was in a jovial mood. By about 1:30 p.m., we headed for the rodeo grounds afoot. We rubbed elbows with quite a few railroaders and ranch hands and never had a bit of trouble. My dad's advice that "you never upset a railroader unless you're close to a hospital" ruled the day. Some idiot driving a '46 Ford pickup pulled up beside Ray Lannen and asked, "Are you idiots riding today or just going down to see the pretty bulls and ponies?"

Ray stopped, looked at the driver, and said, "None of the above. Do we look like idiots, too?"

The driver looked at Ray and said, "Yeah, you four look like real prize winners." He drove off and spun the wheels of the pickup.

Ray shook his fist at the driver, and I just hoped we didn't run into him at the show. If we did, the driver would probably end up with an ambulance escort to the Wheatland County Hospital. All John said was, "That horse's behind could have given us a ride the rest of the way."

Several more cars passed us, and all of the occupants were carrying on some and raising bottles and cans of beer as greetings.

One of them tossed a can of beer to Ray as he went by; Ray caught it, waved back, and said, "At least there's one friendly face in this bunch of spectators."

My brother Tom never said much, and if he had something to say, he usually meant it, but when a brand new Ford car passed us loaded with a whole covey of pretty ladies, he waved his hat and yelled, "I'll see you all later." Seeing five lovely ladies in one herd really shook Tom up. None of us had strings tied to any filly, and we had no desire to tie the loop, but John was still mourning the loss of his lady friend to, as he put it, a fancy dude that never pitched a fork of hay or sat on a horse. He tried something fierce to re-ignite the fire that had suddenly went out, but he never was successful. When I saw her at the rodeo, I could see why he was in mourning. She was as pretty as a red rose, and when she smiled, you just melted.

Sizing up the bulls, and then leaving them alone...

We entered the fair grounds, and after paying at the gate, Ray headed for the chutes, and I tagged along. We passed the meanest looking hump-backed bulls I had ever seen, and they were all carrying on, butting each other and pawing the dirt. They were slobbering at the mouth and bawling like a herd of crazy bulls. Ray and I stood outside the pen and looked them over good.

Ray pulled out a cigarette, stuck it into his mouth, and reached into his shirt for a wooden match. He scratched the match on his Levis, lit the smoke, and took a few puffs. He said, "You know, Al, I probably could stay on that little, black bucking machine for a bit, but I'd probably get a horn through my chest and then croak."

He grinned, flipped the smoke down, and ground it out; we walked down towards the bucking horse pen. Bucking horses are no different than any bunch of horses thrown together. They bite each other, kick at each other, and always move around the pen. Some even try to jump over the fences, and most exhibit scars from spurs, barbwire fences, and interaction with each other, but once the saddle is cinched down tight, they quiet down and tense up, ready for business. When the gate is thrown open, they go nuts, kicking, squealing, and bucking to unseat the rider. The broncs don't like the spurs, and just touching their flanks increases the frenzy of trying to escape—most were successful in unseating their tormentors.

She was the first rodeo lady to become a celebrity...

We watched as bronc after bronc dislodged the riders. A few were ridden for the eight seconds, and a couple riders were given re-rides. Alice Greenough rode a good bucking horse the length of the grounds. Then she dismounted and lifted her arm into the air, and the crowd went plumb crazy—most stood up cheering and yelling her name. What a great treat to see the first rodeo lady to become a celebrity. She was admired and cheered by everyone.

Next came the bareback bronc rides, but it was some tamer than the saddle bronc event. Not too many made the long eight-second ride that seemed a half-hour long. The horses were good buckers, and Ray loved every second of the event.

Each event at the Harlowton rodeo was an exciting contest, but probably the most popular event was the bull riding. When that event began, the clown or, in some cases, clowns carried their colorful, painted barrels into the arena, and the huge crowd cheered and clapped. This was the last event of the rodeo, and in the past, it had been the crowd pleaser. At this rodeo, the bulls were meaner than ever, and one after another, the riders were dumped. Quite a few bulls were able to dislodge the rider right out of the gate, and some took a little longer, maybe four or five seconds. Two of the riders stayed aboard the full eight seconds to the whistle. With the help of the clowns, only one rider was walked on, but didn't appear hurt. One contestant couldn't take his re-ride as he had been gored through the leg. A chute hand told me that the reason bull riding was always last was because last is always best. I have to agree.

The show must go on...

A clown told me once that he mentally rode every bull that came out of the chute with a rider up. He rode the bull right along and always felt a surge of pride if the rider made the whistle for the full eight. He also told me that most injuries happened when the rider was thrown off during the first few jumps and the bull got to him before the clowns could. The worst accidents usually happened when the rider became tangled up with the rope and was thrown around because he couldn't let go.

The clown with the tame buffalo worked his barn paint off, and when the event was over, he rode out on the critter, stopping just outside the gate, and slid to the grass. He leaned up against the fence and lay there, gasping for breath. Ray and I walked over to him and asked if he needed any help. He shook his head, looked at me, and said, "Pneumonia."

He was evidently recovering from an illness and shouldn't have been there. We saw him later in one of the bars, and he told us that the show just had to go on. The event was a great success, and it had to be one of the best July rodeos I had ever seen. We all met Alvin at the Graves Hotel and headed home. It had been a pretty long day.

1947

Brandin' Time

Branding was a hot, dusty, and tiring chore, and one of the top two jobs on every ranch; putting up hay, the other. It all began with four or five cowhands rounding up all of the stock in the spring, pushing them into a holding area, and leaving them overnight to get settled down some. If you have ever looked into the eyes of an overly protective bovine mother, you probably saw distrust and dislike in a massive chuck of hamburger on the hoof just waiting to cause a big ruckus. Branding, dehorning, and performing major surgery on calves caused their watching mothers to get a mite upset with anything wearing boots and jeans—actually, they would probably be content to make a cowhand part of the top soil in the corral.

The prescription was lots of cold beer...

The prescription for a successful branding was lots of cold beer; a few pails of water for various purposes including retrieving all the rocky mountain oysters and cleaning the surgical instruments; a pile of scrap wood; and a good, hot fire to heat the branding irons. The actual crew consisted of a few good ropers, several holders, a fire tender, and a person knowledgeable enough to be able to apply dehorning paste and to use a knife to neuter the cute little bull calves. Also necessary were 12 to 15 onlookers, who were always capable of giving professional advice to everyone. The irons had to be burnt in, which meant heating them red-hot, letting them cool down, and then re-heating them to an almost red glow.

**Al Anderson and horse belonging to Doctor Morledge.
On the Big Elk River by Two Dot, Montana. 1947.**

The calf would run like a turpentined cat...

The ropers would wait patiently for the fire tender to indicate the irons were ready to begin the routine. When everything was all set, he would nod his head, and the cowhands would begin the chore of getting the steers-to-be up to the branding fire. They roped the calf around the neck or feet and drug it over to the fire, where a couple of holders would dump the calf on its side and remove the rope. One holder would grab a hind leg, put his boot just above the knee joint on the other leg, and pull on the top leg while pushing on the bottom one. The other holder would hold the calf's head down while lifting the top leg, and the brander would hit the calf with a hot branding iron. The odor of burning hair and flesh was pretty strong, and when the inner workings were cut off a newly-made steer, the calf would let off a gosh-awful bawl, scramble to his feet, and run like a turpentined cat back to his mother.

Always a few who just couldn't eat their share...

For the uneducated, rocky mountain oysters were a delicious treat if they were deep-fried in butter. But there were always a few observers who just couldn't or wouldn't eat their share. There was usually an over abundance of participants standing around visiting, drinking beer, and trying to look like they knew all about the chore. After a dozen or so new steers were made, quite a few of the onlookers would slowly amble off to get away from the smells, dust, and noise of the animals.

Learning the ways of a good cowhand — the hard way...

In 1945, I worked a branding crew on the lower Musselshell close to where the Musselshell River turned north towards the Missouri. The cowhand who hired me had a 14-year-old son Billy, who was learning the ways of a good cowhand by copying the working hands in the area. It took years of participation in all of the numerous aspects of being a working hand to become a ranch manager.

This 14-year-old cowboy-to-be was involved in every aspect of branding, and he roped and drug a few calves to the branding fire. Billy also took turns holding the future steers, the dehorning paste, and the bucket full of water for the surgery, but they wouldn't let him brand any steers. They had let him brand one calf when he was 13, and he burnt through the hide of the calf, requiring some stitches on the calf. Because he could not handle the branding iron, Billy became a real loud mouth, commented on all the other hands and their abilities, and was sometimes pretty critical.

The little squirt learns a valuable lesson…

We had all taken a break to have lunch, and during the slack time, one of the older hands suggested we ought to teach the little squirt a valuable lesson. We all listened while he expounded on his idea. He told the ropers to leave the oversized brindle calf until the very last, and after all the rest of the calves were taken care of, we'd get Billy to ride that big brindle calf—or at least give him a chance to ride—before we branded him. He said we could all help by bragging on the kid's ability to be a cowboy and offering to let him show all of us just how good he really was. That calf was about 20 pounds heavier than the rest of the batch, and we figured he would unload the kid after about five jumps and prove a point to the kid.

After the break, we all made comments about the kid's exceptional ability and how no one here could ride that calf. We kept telling him that, if anyone could ride that calf to a frazzle, he was just the one to do it. One of the ropers had an extra pair of spurs, and he threw them to the kid, saying, "Put these on; all calves are afraid of spurs." The kid took the spurs to one side and buckled them on, admiring how they looked on his boots.

He jumped three feet straight up in the air…

It wasn't too long before the calves were all branded and taken care of, except the one the kid was going to ride. One of the ropers dropped a rope on the calf and drug him up to the fire. We ran a lasso around his belly, just behind his front legs, and put a rope halter on his head, so the kid could hang on. The calf stood as still as a prairie dog watching a stalking coyote, as we loaded the kid on, handed him the halter rope, and told him to grab the rope around the calf. The kid stuck his free hand under the rope, pulled back on the halter rope, and yelled, "Turn this bull loose!" The calf just stood there for a few moments, so the kid hit him in the flanks with both spurs. Without a doubt, what happened next could probably never be matched. That oversized calf jumped straight up about three feet, kicked his hind feet, and bawled—loud. His mother came charging up while the calf kept raising a pretty good fuss. The kid was hanging on for dear life, white as a Cloroxed sheet, trying to keep his legs around the calf. After about ten seconds, he finally pulled his hand free of the rope and darned near fell off. The calf kicked a few more times and then stopped suddenly, throwing the kid over where he landed right on the back of his lap and bounced a little, sprawled out flat.

Billy, the bull rider...

He scrambled to his feet and took off at a dead run for the fence, the big mother right after him. Billy rolled under the barbed wire fence and lay on the ground a few seconds. Then he reached down, unbuckled the spurs, and threw them at the fire, yelling, "The hell with all of you @#$%!" and walked off towards the barn. We all cheered and whistled as he left the area with his head down. I never saw him again, but I did talk to one of the cowhands who had, and he told me the kid never said too much afterwards, but he did become a pretty good hand during the next few years. Even the moniker, "Billy the Bull Rider," didn't upset him too much. I guess it takes all kinds of experiences to become a good ranch hand.

1944

Chick Wilkinson

During the time I resided in Roundup, Montana—from 1944 through 1950—I worked at various jobs and met some unforgettable and humorous characters who had a never-ending supply of tall tales to tell. One such character was a man named "Chick" Wilkinson. He had worked for years in and around the various mines in Musselshell County and was a man of wide and varied experience. His only fault that I could tell was his constant thirst for strong spirits.

When I first met him, he was working for the Chicago, Milwaukee, St. Paul, and Pacific Railroad that followed the Musselshell River through Roundup. I signed on to work with the section crew in October of 1944, and Chick was sitting in the depot the day I reported for work. The section crew was all waiting for the work bus to take them to their job for the day. Since the duties of the crew varied from day to day, the bus would pick everyone up at the depot at 7:00 a.m. and return them to the depot at 5:00 p.m. The day was spent laying track, mucking out cattle cars, replacing ties, cleaning out gravel cars, and doing a lot of other manual exercise that was necessary to keep the railroad running and on track.

That morning when the bus was ready to leave, we all entered, and Chick sat beside me for the trip. I was new, and I am sure that he wanted to help me break in on the job. I found out that he was about 60 years of age and was just putting in time for the winter on the railroad. On the way to my first job, he told me the following tale that had taken place in the late Twenties.

Chick fell asleep in the grave...

It seems that one of the miners employed at the Klein mine had expired from a combination of bug dust, alcohol, and a small affair with a neighbor's wife, and plans were underway to deliver him to his final resting place, with the grave dug and all preparations completed. The mourning friends adjourned to the closest bar to reminisce and prepare for the event that would take place the following day at 10:00 a.m. in the miners' cemetery. After several hours of recalling the deceased man's many wonderful attributes, the miners started to leave, and Chick started for home in a very happy frame of mind. He lived about one mile from the bar and had to walk past the cemetery. That night, after traveling about twice the normal distance to his house, due to the fact that the path continually tipped up and down, he decided to take a short cut through the cemetery. While walking through the cemetery in the dark, he inadvertently fell headlong into the open grave. He lay stunned for quite a while, and in the interim, it began to rain. He finally gathered his wits and attempted to clamber out of the hole, but due to his delicate condition and the condition of the surrounding dirt caused by the rain, he was unsuccessful. He began to yell and shout, but after about an hour, gave it up and fell asleep.

Sometime during the night, he heard voices near his resting place and shouted out for them to help him out of the hole. He said that complete silence reigned for about ten seconds, and then he heard them running like hell for the boundary of the cemetery. He yelled again, but they were long gone. About daylight, he heard a wagon coming by the cemetery and waited until it was close before yelling for help. As he finished his plea, he heard the horses break into a run and the voice of the driver excitedly urging them on to greater speed.

Dust to dust...

Exhausted and covered with mud, he gave up. Knowing that the services were scheduled for that morning, at which time someone would surely help, he lay down and fell asleep. He slept so sound that, when he awoke, he heard the preacher saying, "Dust to dust." He jumped up and yelled and, in the process, hit his head on the bottom of the coffin, which was about to be lowered into his bedroom. Through the pain, he heard a sound of mass confusion as the funeral participants exited the scene. He yelled again.

For a few minutes he heard absolutely nothing and was about to yell again, when he heard someone say, "Who's there?" Then he saw the preacher's face peering under the casket. He explained what had happened, and the preacher moved the box aside and helped him out of his place of captivity.

Chick told me that it took several hours for the minister to round up the apprehensive mourners from the bars before the service could continue. He also stated that he never took the short cut again. The minister soon left for a church Down South. The story went around that the preacher had been running a close fifth for the first 100 yards before he stopped.

1944

Cushman Dance Hall

Hail to the dance kings and queens and long live the Cushman Orchestra! May the Cushman Dance Hall stand proud forever! During the time I spent in Roundup, Montana, quite a few Saturday nights were enjoyably spent at the Cushman Dance Hall. Cushman, Montana, was a small town west of Roundup situated alongside the Milwaukee Railroad. The town consisted of a few buildings, among which was the Cushman Community Hall—better known as the Dance Hall. The greatest Saturday night dances in Montana were held there, and when anyone mentioned there would be a dance, everyone came. The phrase "dusk 'til dawn" had to be coined just for that dance hall on most Saturday nights. The ladies were all excellent dancers, and the men, most of whom desired to be among those classified as desirable partners, actually were pretty good, too.

Like the cigarette habit, you just had to have another dance...

The Cushman Orchestra consisted of musicians from around the area. With their renditions of the waltz, schottische, and two-step, it was like the cigarette habit—you just had to have another dance. In fact, the Cushman Orchestra was so smooth and inspiring that even Lawrence Welk and Glen Miller had become jealous; at least that was the rumor that started before I came to Roundup in August of 1944. That rumor continued long after I moved away. The band's sound fit together perfectly and attracted quite a few married couples and many more soon-to-be-hitched couples. Some of the manly swains came to the dances well-oiled, and many more left in the same condition. Most of the men brought wine, beer, and various flavors of home squeezin's with them, and everyone was welcome to partake of samples.

The band played loud and became even louder with the decrease of refreshment supply. When quitting time rolled around, usually 2:00 a.m., most participants were either happy, drunk, or somewhere in between. A few drove home down the middle of the road, and the highway patrol would ticket a few—especially those who thought the barrow pit was a part of the highway. And there were always a few who thought they could outrun the Ford V-8s the state patrol used.

Cushman Community Hall. Sketched by Al Anderson.

I attended those dances quite a few times and danced with some of the unattached ladies. It was acceptable to hold your dance partner close, and no one thought anything about it, but I left alone. There was food and refreshments available at midnight, that magic hour when the band took a brief respite. After the band stopped about 2:00 a.m., the exodus began, and most of the dancers arrived home around 3:00 a.m. Some Sunday mornings, there were a few vacancies in the pews.

The winner would win the right of conquest...

I remember one Saturday in May at Cushman when animosity developed over a young lady from Roundup. Two real good friends from Roundup had attended the dance together, and both had danced with the same lady. Their big mistake began when they both partook of some of the home brew that a friend had brought to the dance.

At 2:00 a.m., when the dance ended, they met in the parking lot and by mutual agreement decided to fight. The winner of the fight would win the right of conquest and be the one to escort the lady in question home to Roundup. It seems that she was agreeable and encouraged the fisticuffs for her company.

This young lady, whose name was Joyce, was pretty as a speckled calf and was an excellent dancer. The two competitors for the lady's hand, named Carl and John, were inebriated to the point where standing was a decided chore, and they both weaved back and forth like trees in the wind. They started to circle in an odd sort of way, and suddenly Carl took a swing at John and fell flat on his back. After a few moments, Carl struggled to his feet, and John took a swing at Carl, missed, and fell flat on his face. The spirits and the effort of the fight took too much of a toll on John, and Carl was the winner.

The way John remembered the fight...

I saw John in Kibble & Case the following week, and he had a beautiful black eye. He told me that someone had tripped him and that he fell down during the fight, but he also told me that someone had thrown a rock and hit him in the eye. I never said anything, but I knew the truth. He had landed on a spectator's boot and blackened his eye. After about 15 minutes of chitchat, he told me that the young lady was not so hot after all and that Carl could have her.

The way Carl remembered the fight...

I saw Carl about two months after that, and he told me that the date he had taken home had just married a sailor home on leave. I told him how sorry I was, because she was pretty and was a good dancer. I said I thought they would hit it off. He replied, "By golly, Andy, I just don't understand women. They sure don't think like men. All the time they are smiling at you, they are thinking about how to get someone else—like using you for bait." John and Carl were never friends after that.

L to R: Mona Jean Summers, Al Anderson,
and Evelyn Anderson McCluskey. 1950.

I was content to dance with the cuddly armfuls available, but always left by myself—always, that is, until I met a lovely young lady named Mona Summers. Accompanied by my sister Evelyn and her husband Bill McCluskey, my first date with my future wife was spent dancing at Cushman. Amen!

1951

The Goose

I was sitting by the bunkhouse after the chores were done,
Worrying a hunk of Days O' Work[7], enjoying the Sunday sun,
A peaceful day I'd never seen on this crazy mixed-up spread,
The boss was nuts and his wife was mean as a quart of Dago red.

The old man's wife had a special pet, a big mite-ridden goose,
She kept him locked in a little shed but he kept a-gettin' loose;
He was mean as sin and he hated men and always chased the dog,
Hissin' and flappin' his ragged wings, croaking like a frog.

I'd planned for weeks to fix his goose so the lady wouldn't know,
Like cutting his throat and hiding him good down a six-foot hole;
I swear he knew what I wanted to do 'cause he watched me like a rat,
And when I got close, he'd arch his throat and hiss like a cornered cat.

One day the boss went shopping and took his wife to town,
This was the day I'd fix that goose before the sun went down;
So I was sitting there in that worn out chair when it walked by the door,
And I roped that goose with a hangman's noose and sold him to the store.

1952

---

[7] Chewing tobacco.

Frank's Damascus Shotgun

One Sunday morning in late September of 1945, I opened up Kibble & Case Cigar Store in Roundup, Montana, to get ready for the church-goers who bought their Sunday newspapers from Great Falls and Billings at the store. I was shining up the soda fountain and looked up as the door opened and a rancher walked in. He entered real slow and sat down at the soda fountain in one of the chairs. He pulled a crumpled sack of tobacco and some cigarette papers out of his jacket pocket, spilled a few grains of tobacco onto the paper, and slowly rolled it up into a funny looking cigarette. He lit it with a farmer match, took a couple of puffs, and told me that he would sure like a soda to drink.

He was a little busted up...

His face was not familiar to me, and I looked him over pretty close. He appeared to be about 60 years old, a little bent over, but still a long six feet tall. He had a weather-beaten tan Stetson pushed back on his head and a Levi jacket on over a red shirt that was some wrinkled and in need of soap and water. His hair was scraggly, and his right cheek had a pretty good-sized blister on it that was fairly new. I thought that was the reason he hadn't shaved that day. I fixed up a glass of Coke and put it in front of him, and he put a quarter on the counter. I told him that he was my first customer, and the Coke was free. He picked up the glass, lifted it towards me, and took a good drink. Setting down the glass, he said, "My name's Frank Obert, and I got a little spread down east about 40 miles or so. I've been here since sun up to see Doctor Crouse. He said he'd be here in the morning."

I hadn't noticed his left hand until then, but he lifted it up to the counter, and I saw that a bandage covered the whole hand. I asked him if he had broken his hand, and he told me he had busted it up some. From the way it looked to me, I figured he had been in some kind of accident or car wreck. I looked out the big window at his pickup, and it wasn't bashed up at all.

There ain't nothing that's ever cut and dried...

Frank looked at me and said, "There ain't nothing that's ever cut and dried. This darn accident started Saturday morning when I told Bess, my wife, that I was going into Melstone to borrow a gun and buy some shells. My boy had taken my 12 gauge with him when he went to Missoula to school. I wanted to pop a few pheasants to eat. She said okay and asked me to pick up a few things at the store. She gave me a list of stuff she needed, which I planned to bring back. When I got to the store, my old friend was gone for the day, so I couldn't get the gun. The storekeeper told me one of the men on the section crew had a shotgun he had been trying to sell, but nobody wanted it. He said the fella wanted $20 for the gun. It was an old eight gauge that had to be loaded through the barrel.

I told Frank that it was probably an old muzzleloader that used black powder and that, more than likely, it had a Damascus barrel.

He just looked at me kind of funny and said, "I didn't care if the thing was made in Timbuktu. If the darn thing could shoot, I aimed to buy it and head on home."

They'd get along fine with their Sears and Roebuck catalogue...

Frank had pulled out Bess' list, and all that was on it was some spuds and some toilet paper. The clerk got the spuds and then told him that all they stocked was bath tissue. He asked her what in the devil did you use tissue for in a tub full of hot water? What the heck, even he knew that you didn't use tissue paper in water and that not even an old Sears and Roebuck catalogue could be used like that. The clerk turned pink, got mad, and offered to rip off a bunch of butcher wrap for him free of charge. Frank looked at that stuff and it was slick as oilcloth on one side, so he told her they'd get along with their Sears and Roebuck catalogue. I wondered about him when he told me that.

It could tickle the tail feathers on any pheasant...

Frank said, "I found out where the railroader lived and drove over to see about the gun. He was an older guy, maybe purt' near 70, and he told me his dad had given him the gun over 50 years ago, and it had been used quite a lot. It had a crack in the stock, was a little rusty, and was a muzzleloader. The guy told me that that old gun could reach out and tickle the tail feathers on any pheasant at over 60 feet. He showed me how to load the gun using black powder. He had a stick of black powder that he cut open with a pocketknife. He dumped a handful of BBs down the barrel on top of the rag and shoved another piece of cloth down on top of that. He picked up a long stick and thumped it down the barrel pretty good—he said, "to set it."

"Now I ain't stupid," Frank continued, "I got through the eighth grade real handy, and I've shot black powder guns, but they shot a little round ball. When the gun fired, a cloud of blue smoke bellowed out of the gun. I figured that his gun was about the same.

"We went out to the porch, and the guy showed me an old milk can about 100 feet off. He took a copper cap out of a little can he had and put it on the little nipple under the hammer. He cocked the gun, handed it to me, and told me to try it out. I aimed at the can and pulled the trigger, and the milk can rolled a few feet away. After the cloud of smoke cleared so I could see, I saw a brown chicken lying beside the milk can. I felt that the gun was what I needed, and I gave him $20 for the gun and all the supplies. I threw them into the pickup and headed back to home. On the way back, I saw quite a few pheasants along the roadway, and I stopped to see if I could get a couple for dinner."

Old Frank was bleeding like a chopped chicken...

I fixed Frank another Coke, and he drank about half of it. Then he said, "I sat on the side of the road and followed the loading instructions, dumping in a good handful of powder and the rest of the BBs. I put a chunk of Levi jacket down on top of the load. Then I put a cap on the nipple and cocked the gun. As I was walking, I stumbled on some loose gravel and dropped the gun. It hadn't fired, so I picked it back up and walked along the road looking for birds. A couple flew up so I aimed the gun and pulled the trigger."

He looked at me for a moment and rubbed his cheek with his bandaged hand. Then he said, "The next thing I knew I was laying on the road about three feet from the gun, bleeding like a chopped chicken, and I thought I had been hit by a truck or a mad bull. I looked at my left hand, and I only had three fingers left. It was squirting blood, so I used an old rag I had to wrap up my hand. I picked up the gun, threw it in the pickup, and headed back to Melstone. The clerk in the drug store put some salve on my face, which was burned pretty bad, and bandaged my hand so I wouldn't bleed to death. I got here at 4:00 o'clock this morning, and I'm waitin' to see the doc. Sundays are a bad time to get hurt."

I asked him where the gun was, and he said, "I'll go get it and show you." He went out to the pickup and brought in a mangled gun with the barrel almost unwound. I could see what had happened. When he pulled the trigger, the two things that caused it to explode were easy to see: too much black powder and a barrel full of dirt from falling on the ground.

The Damascus barrel was made by winding red-hot wire around a round shaft and annealing the wire into a solid barrel with force. It had unwound like a spring, taking his little finger in the process and heating the barrel so hot it burned his cheek. When he dropped the gun, it probably forced the barrel full of mud and, plugging up the end of the barrel, left no place else for the charge and the BBs to go but through the wound barrel. I told him he was lucky that he still had his hand and both eyes. Frank went out the door to his pickup.

The next time Dr. Crouse came into the store, I asked him about Frank. All he said was, "Ya, he came up to the office, and I fixed him up. His little finger was chopped off right next to the knuckle. I don't think he'll miss it too much. He'll probably eat a bunch of aspirin for the pain, but he'll be okay."

I'll never forget that Sunday morning in September.

1945

Frenchy, Cowboy by Choice

In 1945, I was working at Kibble & Case Cigar Store in Roundup, Montana, and had become acquainted with most of the stockmen, sheep men, and farmers in and around Musselshell County. I also met quite a few rodeo riders and bulldoggers that rode the small town circuit every year as long as they could. During the time I spent in Roundup, I ingested an awful lot of information about cowhands and sheep men from itinerant cowhands who worked a month and were gone the next. I listened to a great many tales of the early times and some of the hardships, accidents, and successes of riders of the open range.

I knew that some of those stories were embellished to a large degree, some were total baloney, some were almost true, but only a few were gospel fact. The habit of injecting items into true stories made them sound great, but sure as the devil, ruined their historical value. I kept notes on the ones that I thought were close to being factual and that I was assured were true to the extent of the teller's knowledge and ability. Those stories about bronc riders and cowboys usually had a small ray of humor along with the positive and loud declaration that they were gospel.

Cowboy history as spun by an old ranch hand...

Hap Kibble told me that, if I believed anyone, it should be the cowhands, as they were not prone to spread rumors about anyone and usually had first-hand knowledge of what they yarned about. I made notes over a period of several visits with an itinerant cowhand named Harold Moffert, who had worked on a spread or two north of the Musselshell, about a yarn concerning a Frenchman named Renaldo "Frenchy" Bernardae. Moffert had worked with Frenchy one fall rounding up cattle and told me bits and pieces of the cowboy's history, some of his working life, and his final job on the range in eastern Montana.

He figured he would be hired because he was a gentleman...

Around 1880, Frenchy, then 18 years of age, had come out West on the Union Pacific Railroad with a friend, and they hoped to get hired as cowboys on a large ranch. They had exited the train at a small town called Cheyenne and roosted there for a couple of weeks to get used to the area and find out where the best ranches were. Being French, Frenchy figured that most ranchers would hire him because he was a gentleman and a hard worker. He had a solid family history, but he had none of the required skills of a cowboy or even a horse wrangler, though he could ride a horse. He didn't know how to scorch a brand into the hide of a calf, make steers out of little bulls, do any kind of ranch upkeep, or even cook steaks. But he was there, and some ranchers were having trouble finding cowboys who would do the hardest work in Wyoming for $15 a month. Those who did were extremely mobile and hard to keep.

The ranchers were just beginning to lay claim to the rolling acres of open range and were putting up fences to keep their cattle from going every which way, because it required an awful lot of effort to round them up. Frenchy and his friend, one Poirott De Lanes, rode a rented buggy around the area and tried several of the big ranches and were turned down by the foremen, until they pulled into a small spread up by Laramie ran by an old trail driver with a few cowhands. The ranch was not too far from Fort Casper. Both men were hired, with Poirott hired as a general hand to help the cook and do other odd jobs around the ranch, and Frenchy hired to be a working cowhand if possible; if not, they would run him off in the fall.

The other hands had trouble saying the name Poirott, so they nicknamed him Porridge, and the name stuck. One old hand, who was asked why the name "Porridge," said, "What the hell, he works in the cook shack, don't he?"

Red shirt or not, he had the makin's of a hand...

The old boss was Will Ragland, and he was a crusty old mule rider. Frenchy told Will that he was an excellent rider and had grown up on the back of thoroughbred stock. A couple of weeks later, after Frenchy got the lay of the land (including which way was north), he was told the next morning he was to ride the line fence to make sure that no one had tore it down and run off with any cows. At sun up, Frenchy came out of the bunkhouse wearing a bright red shirt, new Levis, new boots, and a ten-gallon hat. He saddled up one of the remuda and started off to the west, riding straight and tall in the saddle. That, being his first chore, was a trial run, and the foreman figured it would take him three to four hours to get the job done, so he should be back by five at the latest.

Frenchy never returned, and as it got dark, the foreman told one of the older hands to start out early the next morning and see if Frenchy had been bucked off and got stranded or had been hurt too bad to ride. They all expected the worst, and they figured the pony had stepped into a hole, broke a leg, and hurt the Frenchman bad.

In the early days, building fence on the range was a hard, long, and dangerous chore, and most times a cowhand would quit and ride off rather than handle the barbwire and end up cut all over. A lot of fencing was built on Jack fence, which resembled a series of sawhorses like jacks with wire strung between them. The plains looked flat and smooth, but there were outcroppings of rocks and sandstone that had to be crossed to keep the cattle corralled. If the rider's horse had fallen into one of those rock piles or into the fence, it would be a tough way to get hurt.

The rider sent to look for Frenchy had left at daybreak, riding at a slow trot to favor the horse. After riding about two hours, the cowhand found a hole in the Jack fence, and searching the ground, the evidence indicated that a bunch of cows had departed the area through the downed fence and headed towards the Platte River. On top of the cattle tracks were the tracks of a lone horse heading in the same direction. The river was about 20 miles or so away, and the rider followed the cow tracks north for quite a ways. Along about dark he came over a low hill, and there, right below the hill, was a herd of about 30 cows, all in a bunch. As he looked around, he saw a red-shirted cowhand riding slowly around the cattle, keeping them close together. He rode down the hill and up to the red-shirted rider and yelled at Frenchy, who was tickled no end to see him ride up.

Frenchy said he had been riding along when he came to a stretch of downed fence and saw a bunch of cows on the other side. They wore Ragland's brand so Frenchy had circled them to bunch them together. He had circled the cows all night to keep the wolves and coyotes away and had just started to push them back towards the downed fence when the other rider showed up. Together they pushed the stock up to and through the downed fence and managed to stand the fence up with some rocks. They returned to the ranch, and when the foreman heard the whole story of what the Frenchman had been able to accomplish on his own, he was well pleased. Frenchy became a fixture on the ranch and worked there several years.

He caught a disease common to cowboys in those days...

Frenchy finally caught a disease called "Wanderlust," and one morning he just saddled up his horse and headed up towards Sheridan, Wyoming, to join an outfit driving a herd of cattle to Bozeman to feed the soldiers and miners. From that job, Frenchy rode east and up towards Fort Benton on the Missouri River, just riding the grub line. He worked a while on a sheep ranch west of Roundup, a small town on the Musselshell, and spent some time riding down the Yellowstone River area, ending up in Fort Keogh. He landed in Lewistown that fall and later accepted a roundup job up by Havre, Montana, close to the Canadian border. He met quite a few cowpunchers, some who were riding with a loose rope along the Missouri breaks. He made friends with a small encampment of Crow Indians resting on the flats east of the Musselshell River. He also worked a roundup just north of the Musselshell River and pushed a small herd of cows, along with three other punchers, down to Fort Keogh in eastern Montana.

When you sign on, you know the risks...

When winter came on early that year, Frenchy was working on a small spread east of Sand Springs. A snowstorm began in the middle of December on a cold Saturday afternoon, and the wind came up from the east—a stinging, blustery, dark day. The wind, coming off the plains of the Big Bend of the Musselshell, piled the snow against the fences, covering every clump of sagebrush and small brush so they looked like igloos. Frenchy had been sent out through a part of the range to make sure the cows didn't pile up in the coulees and freeze to death trying to keep warm. He was due back before dark and had been told to tie one of his pony's reins to his arm, just in case the horse spooked.

As day ran into night, Frenchy never returned, and the blizzard was so intense that no one could ride out to try to find him. The storm blew out after three days of constant wind and snow, and finally two riders set out to see if they could find Frenchy. They did find him in a macabre setting froze to death. He was lying with his arms stretched out with a newborn calf beside him. His neckerchief was wrapped around the calf's nose like a mask, and the calf was laying on his right side. From all appearances, Frenchy had found the calf and dismounted to pick him up, and his horse bolted. He had evidently tried to carry the calf to shelter, but there just wasn't any. It appeared that he had tried to shield the little calf because his sheepskin coat was unbuttoned. Snow 24 inches deep covered all the prairie, and there would have been no hope of making the long distance to the ranch.

That spring when the thaw began, they found 11 head of cattle, several with their feet in the air, frozen hard as a rock. A couple of weeks later, when they rode by that coulee, there were only bones left by the wolves and coyotes, as a memento of the disaster. Frenchy's horse was found about a mile from where he bolted, lying halfway across part of downed fence. Evidently, the horse had tried to jump the fence, got hung up, and froze to death. His back legs were wound with barbwire, and a broken cedar post lay beside him. He had evidently run along the fence, came to a low fence wire, and got caught. All of Frenchy's gear was intact on the horse.

The price was high, settling the West...

They buried Frenchy behind the ranch house and marked the grave with a wood cross. When they cleaned out his bunk and opened his possibles sack, they found a $20 gold coin, an old gun (like new), a handful of shells, and a tintype picture of an attractive lady who they assumed was either his mother or sister because she resembled Frenchy. Under his mattress, they found a pair of jeans, a pair of socks, and a shirt in pretty good condition with all of the buttons intact. There was a letter dated 1898 mailed from England in the pocket of the shirt. The foreman took the letter and mailed it back with a short note on the accident.

Frenchy was a dedicated working cowhand, born in 1862 in London, England. He took his final ride on the prairie in eastern Montana on December 24, 1904. After 42 years on the open range, he had left no known relatives. His gear was put in a small shed, just in case anybody showed up to claim it. In 1937, a range fire destroyed the shed and its contents. That was it.

1945

George Francis, Cowboy & Rustler

In July of 1944, a rancher named Elmer Hinton, who raised blooded horses, borrowed me from Kibble & Case in Roundup for a weekend to help him put up some hay in his horse barn out north of Roundup. When we finished putting up the hay, a mix of wild grass, thistles, willows, and some sagebrush, I went over to his well by the cabin and sat there cooling off for a spell. Elmer had just finished currying his cutting horse named Big Red, and he had brought a couple of bottles of beer over, so we drank some as we recouped. We were just sitting there, quiet-like, because

Elmer was not prone to do much talking. After we had drunk a few sips, Elmer took off his old sweat-stained Stetson, laid it on its top on the ground, and sat his beer in the hat.

In a man of few words, thanks meant a lot...

Elmer looked at me intently for a few moments and then said, "I'll take you to town in the morning, and I really appreciate your help." He handed me a $20 bill and said, "Here, 'til you're better paid."

I had heard my dad use that term, and I knew it meant he would pay me more if he had it. We sat there a while longer, enjoying the slight breeze from the west and just loafing.

After a half hour, Elmer finished his beer and laid the bottle across his lap. He said, "Andy, have you ever been up to Havre, along the top of the state? It's up above the Missouri Breaks towards Canada."

I told him no but that my dad had worked for the Great Northern Railroad and had been there a few times. I said that he had told me some tales about the town but I didn't pay much attention to them. One thing Dad did say was that, at one time, a lot of rustlers and thieves had roosted in the area, but they had been rounded up and killed.

George was the kind of man folks just trusted...

Elmer looked at me and then said, "Did you ever hear the story about a cowhand named George Francis?" I didn't recognize the name, and I told him no. Elmer said he always figured that someday, someone would come onto his spread and run off a few head of horses, but they never did. After talking about a few of the older brands, like the 2 Dot, N Bar, 2 Bar, 79, and the 7-7, Elmer told me the following yarn while sitting in the shade of his old two-room house. It was tale about a good cowhand turned bad named George Francis.

George Francis was a product of Utah and a wanderer, leaving Utah and going up into Idaho to work for a cattle outfit called the War Bonnet. He ended up in Montana with a herd of War Bonnet cattle and worked for them until they ceased operation about 1895.

He also worked for the YT Brand, rodeoed some, and found time to brand quite a few stray doggies. He was known to be around when quite a few horses went missing from some of the spreads. He was figured to be a horse thief and was jailed for a spell.

In an odd twist, he later spent some time in law work as a policeman in Havre. Later on, he partnered up with a man named Richel, and together they ran a ranch west of Havre called the Hook Ranch. He was a big fella and real good at riding broncs and bulldogging in rodeos. He was the kind of man people liked and trusted—a so-called good cowhand.

George probably could have gotten elected as Governor...

Elmer had first heard of George when he was working rodeos; George was so well-liked that he probably could have ran for Governor and got elected. But then one day a horse of Earl Clack's went missing, and George was charged with rustling. I think that was in 1916 or '17, and he was tried a year later or so and found guilty as sin. He ended up in the Crowbar Hotel where he had some friends bail him out. When they opened the cell door, George took off for the tall timber. They put a bounty on him, about $500, and flooded the state with wanted posters. Elmer had one of the flyers that was put out by the state brand inspector.

It was about a year later that George turned himself in, and the judge sentenced him to ten years in jail. Again, some of his friends bailed him out. George was supposed to go to prison in December of 1920, and according to the news from Hill County, he never got to the prison, but instead died in the Milk River. It seemed that he had wrecked his car, ended up in the river which was mostly frozen over, and died trying to get out. One of the local ranchers found him, and they buried him in the local cemetery. It was said that rustling died out after that, and everyone said he probably was the rustler.

Good horseflesh was ranked right up there with a good woman...

Elmer said that an awful lot of cowhands ranked good horseflesh right up there with a good woman and worth every bit of a herd of yearling cows. Elmer and I spent the rest of the day looking for the wanted poster, but we never found it. Elmer figured the mice got it. I knew Elmer well enough to know he wasn't fabricating anything, so I told him I'd look into the story when I had the time, but I never seemed to find the time to do that.

Elmer was one great horseman, and I used to see him quite a bit. He was the hardest working old rancher I ever met. He still raises horses out under the Big Wall, north of Roundup.

1945

Gus Rehder

In September of 1944, the war in Europe was still ripping countries apart, and the Nazis were eliminating all people they considered undesirables. The greater share of those eliminated were of Jewish descent. The tide of war had turned a bit by the fall of 1944, and the Allies could forecast victory over the Nazis. Montana wasn't rejoicing much in that progress because the shortages of food, clothing, gasoline, and other necessary items continued to cause real hardships. A good share of the local miners traipsed through Kibble & Case and blamed the war for all of their problems: from the shortage of cigarettes, to headaches, sore muscles, and problems with their feet because of the shoe shortage.

From time to time, Hap Kibble would get his fill of the repetitive bitching, and just as he was getting ready to walk home to have supper, he would pick up his jacket and, before he put it on, he would address the normally crowded store. He told them all to go and get their guns, and he'd pay for the bus fare for them to go and fight the dirty s.o.b.s causing all of their problems. One miner usually spoke out and said something like, "Hell, Hap, we'd all be willing to go, but you ain't got no ammunition to give out for us to fight with."

Hap would stand there thinking about that, and then he'd say, "See, I told you guys so. If you'd get any ammunition, you'd probably just go shoot prairie dogs for supper." Then he'd pull on his coat and go out the door, and all the patrons would laugh and say, "Poor old Hap."

181

I didn't side with anyone, and I kept my mouth shut until Hank Brookman would come in to replace Hap. I just figured that they were entitled to their thoughts and opinions; besides, most of them were tougher than an undercooked steak cut off a 20-year-old range bull fed strictly on sagebrush. Everyone faced the same problems and shortages, and no one could do anything about it.

Hap had a firearms license, but couldn't get any guns to sell. He did have an old 12-gauge shotgun that he rented out for $5 a day. We would also get a small allotment of .22 shells, but we had to register everyone who bought a box of 50—that was all they could buy. It seemed like everyone who bought a box complained about the government. More than once, I turned down $5 a box if I would sell more than one. I always made sure that all customers were treated the same. I came to know all of the ranchers and miners that walked through the door.

One week in September of 1944, Hap was heading towards Billings, Montana, for a Shriners' meeting. He told me that, under no circumstances—bribery, threats of violence, or retribution—was I to break any of the rules that Kibble & Case operated on. We had just received 20 assorted cartons of cigarettes, delivered by Elwood, the manager of the Miles City Mercantile Company.

Most men smoked, and we had many customers from other towns trying to buy anything with tobacco in it. I sold to dentists, bankers, doctors, ranchers, miners, a few housewives, and railroad men. Some would make the rounds every Friday, hoping to stock up if they could. Everyone who worked at our store smoked, and we always had plenty of tobacco for our own use. Copenhagen, Beechnut, Red Man, W-B Cut, Star, Days O' Work, and a few other brands of chewing tobacco were always in stock. Smoking tobacco was plentiful in packages, tins, and sacks. Bull Durham, Half and Half, Edgeworth, Golden Grain, and Peerless were the most sought-after brands. Sales of tobacco products were good, and it seemed that everyone who came into the store used tobacco of one kind or the other.

Sounds an awful lot like Russia...

As 1944 slid down towards 1945, I met a rancher named Gus Rehder, who ranched up in the Bull Mountains south of Roundup. Gus and his wife, Mae, were good, solid Western folk. Gus came into Kibble's one Saturday and asked me if we had any .22 shells left. I told him that we did and that I could sell him one box of 50. Then I told him that he had to sign the record book. He pushed his Stetson back on his head and said, "I figured there'd be some kind of record on who bought what. One of these days, the government will know where everyone lives, what they do to live, how many kids they got, and what they're worth. Sounds an awful lot like Russia to me." I didn't say anything, and he asked, "Would you sell my wife a box of shells if I sent her in later?" Later on the day, Mae came in, and I sold her a box of 50, too.

Gus came into the store off and on and would take time to visit with me about the weather, the war, the mining going on, and business in general. I found out he was 74 years young, and he seemed to get more wrinkles every trip, like he had stared at the sky from under the brim of his Stetson for too long. Just before Christmas, Gus came into the store, and we visited for quite a while. It had snowed some and was colder than a well digger's ears, and he wasn't in a hurry to leave.

Remembering the old times...

As a young man, Gus had met an older, big, grey-headed man at Fort Maginnis up in the Judith Basin, who ramrodded a spread with the DHS brand and ran a good-sized herd of cattle. Gus was only 14 years old at the time, and he figured that he might work up there one day. He told me he later got the job and got to know quite a few hands, among them men named O'Donnell and Abbott, and he had seen Charlie Russell from over Utica way. He also knew about a group of riders called the "Stranglers," who had hung quite a few rustlers they had corralled in the area.

I left Kibble & Case later that year and never got the opportunity to visit with Gus again. He passed on in 1947. Mae eventually sold the ranch to a man named Johnson and opened a bar in Farrell Town named "The First and Last Chance Saloon." Mae ran the bar for a few years, but I lost track of her in 1950. Gus and Mae were good ranchers. People like them left a big mark on the area and made the Roundup area a great place with all its history. If only one of them had written down some of their trials and tribulations, what an interesting story it would make. The actual history of Roundup and the Musselshell area would tell much about ranching in Montana.

1950

Autumn

The many colors of turning leaves
Lend their beauty to the trees;
And the gradual dying of the grass
Comes unheeded as summer hurries past.

The stubbled fields and shocks of corn
Enhance the biting crispness of the morn;
The diluted rays of a once-hot sun
Leave many summer chores undone.

The exotic moon in fullness stays
Among the brittle stars that gaze
Upon the subdued world below
Where now contentment seems to grow.

The beauty of this Autumnal world
Lies still, with golden fields unfurled
To ripple wave-like in the breeze,
A reward to man, his labor eased.

1952

Hard Tack Bill

A rancher and a close friend of mine when I lived in Roundup, Montana, was Frank Kombol. He ranched northwest of Roundup in the Jones Creek area with two brothers and his mother. Frank was ten years older than I was and was unmarried when I knew him. He drove into Roundup several times a week and spent a lot of time at Kibble & Case visiting with me. Most of our conversations concerned early Roundup, especially the '20s and '30s. He used to say, "The early 1900s were the harsh and hungry times." He was born in the year 1918 and had acquired a lot of knowledge by word of mouth of the early days in and around Roundup. He told me that the winters in the early 1900s were terrible, and any glamour of being a cowboy was non-existent. He claimed it would have been easier to punch cows at the North Pole.

Finally, the politicking was over…

One Saturday in December, Frank came into the store, and we visited for quite a while. He told me about a rancher named Hightower that was one of the first cattlemen in the area. Hightower had trailed a bunch of cattle from western Montana to the Roundup area and had some pretty good cowhands on his payroll.

He said that one of Hightower's men was a young cowboy called Hard Tack Bill. His given name was Henry Porter Hinton, and he had driven some cattle up into Montana as a trail boss at 21 years of age in 1871. The cows carried the 7U brand, and Bill had ten trail hands to work the ornery longhorns. They threw the herd on the flats in the area where Buffalo, Montana, is situated, and built a small cabin along the Musselshell River, just a few miles from where Judith Gap now stands.

Frank said that they were pretty successful for a while. One day, when they were rounding up cows for branding, Bill's horse was lame so he had borrowed a friend's mare named Flame. The horse walked too close to a rattlesnake, and in jumping away from it, stepped into a prairie dog burrow and broke its leg. Bill got dumped into some rocks and ended up with two broken legs and a shattered hip. They had to shoot the horse, and that fall ended Bill's riding days. He was 42 years old in 1892.

Bill spent several weeks in bed fighting with the nearest vet (doctor) about being able to get back to work with cows. He finally healed up some, but was confined to the cook shack as head cook. Frank said that Bill's first day as a cook was worse than quicksand in the middle of the river. The cook he had replaced had gone to town, got drunk, and stayed drunk for a week. Bill cussed that cook for leaving him to perform miracles with a wood stove. All that the cook left behind was a sack of potatoes, a chunk of bacon, and a pan full of eggs. Cowboys ran on meat, potatoes, bread, and coffee, but according to Bill, all he knew how to cook was coffee and beans.

The first morning, Bill said he had to feed nine hungry cowhands, and he panicked. He found the largest cast iron skillet in the cookhouse and built up a roaring fire. He found three dozen eggs and broke them into the skillet. He found a three-pound chunk of greenish bacon that he cut up, and he threw a cup of hog fat into the pan, too. While that was cooking, he found three old stale loaves of bread in a tin box that he cut up and put on the table. When he figured the eggs were about done, he rang the dinner bell. Bill said he was almost run over by the hungry cowpokes as they came dashing in the cook shack. Bill said the mess smelled good, and the men ate everything on the table. They all gave him the business about how bad the food tasted, but all he said to them was, "If the grub tasted that bad, how come you ate it all?"

Bill said he sat down at the table when all the hands had left and thought about quitting, but he didn't, and come spring, he stocked up the chuck wagon and worked the roundup. He had a helper who was a friend of Frank's. Bill told the helper a bunch of stories about the old days, cattle drives, and roundups.

Everyone soon came to treat old Bill with the utmost respect, and he gradually became the cook, doctor, confidante, and advisor to all the cowhands. He ran his last wagon on the roundup in 1897.

The cowboys mostly wore all the clothes they owned, every day...

Frank told me that the summers back then were hotter than a mouse's foot on a wood stove. The ritual of bathing in the spring, after a long, cold winter spent wearing long johns, was religiously followed by most cowhands. After all, there was no running water except the creek, and it was frozen over all winter. Peeling off the old long johns was harder than taking the skin off a grape.

The old dependable out-house was always ten less degrees than the temperature outside, but it never froze up, and the mail order catalogues provided lots of entertainment for the patrons to help ease the cold. Old Bill kept that think tank well supplied with reading material. That way the hands knew what was available every year.

According to Frank, some winters were so cold and growly that quite a few coyotes froze in mid-step and stood around like statues until the spring thaw when they could continue on their journey.

Sometimes it was so cold that water pulled from the well froze on the way up and had to be thawed in the cook shack. A few times the rope that pulled the water bucket up froze so hard it wouldn't wrap around the pulley to even get fresh water. All winter Bill kept his deep freezer and old wagon box covered with a tarp, full of ham and beef.

Some summers, it was so hot you could make coffee just by throwing a handful of coffee grounds into your Stetson, adding some water, and setting into a pan to boil. The sun did the rest.

Cowhands had to ride the range the year around and usually wore all the clothes they owned every day, especially in the winter. However, they did remove their spurs at night. Old Bill had a pair of cowhide chaps that he wore every day and sometimes even to bed. Bill died in bed on the ranch when he was 58 years old. He was buried on a small hill just below an old pine tree he loved to sit under in the summer.

Frank remarked that, later that night, a coyote sat by the tree and mourned until daylight. The next morning the coyote was gone and never seen again. Frank said that sometimes he almost believed in reincarnation because he had seen lots of prairie dogs that looked like some of the older cowhands.

Frank Kombol died of cancer in 1991.

1946

Henry Mervin Shenkel, Bronc Rider

I became acquainted with Hank Shenkel one morning in 1944, while helping Elmer Hinton put up hay at Elmer's horse ranch out in the Big Wall country north of Roundup. I had agreed to help Elmer put in some cured hay in the middle of August, and I planned to stay out there until the first part of September. The term "putting in hay" meant filling up the loft in a small barn where Elmer kept some of his horses. "Stacking hay" meant building big piles of loose hay out in the hayfield. Elmer had some Thoroughbred horses he kept in a corral and attached barn and he fed them hay and oats year round.

He said he was the best bronc rider in Montana...

Elmer and I were out in the hayfield when this man rode up, hat pushed back on his head and an unlit, hand-rolled smoke dangling from the side of his mouth. The sorrel horse he was riding was about 15 hands high and more than ten years old. His horse was well shod, well groomed, and alert. His saddle was an old center fire rig, but it was well-oiled and in real good condition. He sat straight in the saddle, and when he came riding up to Elmer, I could see that he was pushing 50 years and they hadn't been extra kind to him. His face was deeply lined and looked like brown leather—he had looked into the sun some, and the dry wind-blown prairie sun took its toll. When he came closer, he reined up, hooked an almost worn-out boot over the saddle horn, and looked at Elmer. He picked the unlit smoke out of his mouth, flipped it away, and said, "Howdy, my name's Henry Shenkel, but all of my friends call me Hank."

We shook hands all around, and Elmer asked, "What in the devil are you doing way out here?"

Hank looked at Elmer and said, "I heard you were raisin' Quarter Horses, and I'm the best bronc rider in Montana if you need some broncs wore down to ride. I can gentle any horse born and any green bronc you own. When I'm through with a horse, mare or stud, even a little grey-haired old lady could ride it to church, feed it out of her hand, and saddle it all by herself. Right now, I'm thirsty, drier than a two-hump camel in the middle of the desert, and we could use a drink. My horse's last water was in the Musselshell down by Melstone!"

Elmer nodded at the pump and told him to fill up. After watering his horse, Hank stood at the well and downed two or three cups of water. Elmer and I finished filling the hayrack, and when we stopped for a moment, Hank came over and visited with Elmer for a few minutes. Pretty soon, Hank mounted up and rode off toward the house and corral. He rode like he was part of the saddle and sat straight and tall.

Ten dollars is a bargain to break that stud...

I looked at Elmer, and he was rolling a cigarette, Bull Durham sack dangling from his mouth by the yellow string, and watching Hank ride back to the house. After a moment, he lit the cigarette and took a puff. Then he said, "He looks like a bronc rider. I took him on to break a big, ornery stud I ain't been able to reason with. Ten dollars is pretty cheap to break any bronc, but it's a bargain for that stud." That was the most conversation I had heard from Elmer since I met him. He was usually real quiet and seldom said more than a few words.

Hank knew all kinds of stories...

That night at supper, Hank was eager to visit, and we talked about rodeos he had been in and horses that he had rode—or at least tried to ride. I asked him a lot of questions and found out that he was an old rodeoer on the small town circuit, which included

Lewistown, Roundup, Red Lodge, Big Timber, and Harlowton. He had also spent a few weekends in Miles City and Glendive.

He was tall and thin and walked with a limp from a past broken hip. His prized possessions consisted of a pair of reading glasses, a bedroll, an old black powder pistol he kept wrapped in his Sunday shirt in his saddlebags, and a bone-handled two-blade pocketknife. He said the knife was for picking out cactus spines he sometimes picked up from sleeping on the ground.

One of his stories was about a rodeo rider in Great Falls, Montana, who rode and won second money with a fractured leg. Another was about a rider that grabbed a pretty good-sized steer by the horns but his hands slipped off the horn. In the process, he was gored through the thigh, but went on to place later in the day in bull dogging.

**Al Anderson.
September, 1948.**

Elmer's coffee was the only thing stronger than the stud...

The evening went by quickly, and it seemed even shorter because Hank was up at dawn and out by the corral, looking over the stud that Elmer wanted broke. I grabbed a cup of coffee and hurried out to the corral to see what was going on. I figured that Hank was going to start breaking the stallion, and I wanted to see all the action. Hank was in the corral trying to talk his way up to the horse, but each time he got within a few steps, the horse would shy away. All the time Hank was talking to the horse, he was whistling real soft through his front teeth. That went on for about a half-hour with no success. Then Hank walked over to his saddle and pulled his rope off, twirled it a couple of times, and roped the stud. The horse reared up, but Hank threw a loop over the snubbing post in the center of the corral and pulled the rope as tight as he could so the stud couldn't move about too much. Then Hank pulled his saddle off the corral rail and carried it over to the center post.

Hank stood there for a few moments, studying the stud, and then motioned for me to help him put a blindfold on the now calm horse. I'd seen quite a few horses broke to ride growing up, and Hank was following all the right moves that I had seen many times before. I figured then that he would be the winner of the next round. I moved slowly up to the stud and grabbed the rope, and Hank moved up right behind me and grabbed the rope. I dropped my share of the rope and grabbed the sack from Hank. We finally got the blindfold on the stud, and it was like trying to hand feed a wolverine. He reared up, pawed the air, and made noises like a grizzly bear. It was just one heck of a fight. I held on to the horse's head while Hank gently threw the saddle on, and we had another swirling fight as Hank tried to tighten the cinch. When he finished that, he cut the rope loose with his knife, leaving about six feet to hang on to. Hank retied the rope to the center post and the stud calmed down some, just moving a few steps. He finally stood still, snorting with flared nostrils and quivering just a bit. He was a bit nervous and not one bit happy.

Hank stood looking at the stud, smoking on a cigarette for about five minutes. Finally, he looked at me and said, "He's one mean piece of horse. He thinks he's tougher than he is. Let's just leave him stand there for a while and go get a cup of coffee. That's the only thing I know of that's stronger than that horse."

That dirty s.o.b. tricked me...

We went and had some coffee and returned to the corral. After removing every item that could hurt the horse or Hank, we slowly approached the stud. Hank held on to the rope, talking in a soft voice, and petting the horse's mane in a gentle, easy way. After a few minutes, Hank said to me, "I'm climbing aboard now and when I do, pull the rope off the snubber and toss it to me, quick like. Then pull the gunny sack from his head and move back." He waited a few more moments and then mounted the horse, and I threw him the rope off the post. That stud stood plumb still, quivering like a goat passing plum seeds, not making a sound. Then he pulled back from the post, reared up on his hind legs, and tried to get out from under Hank. Hank's saddle was a center rig, and I just knew that the cinch would break or the saddle would do a 180-degree turn and end up under the stud.

Hank was yelling some unkind words at the stud and spurring him pretty good at every jump. The stud bucked all the way around the corral, squealing some and trying to get his head down. When he came to the gate I was standing on, he planted all four feet, slid to a halt, turned his head to the right, and bucked once more. I could see the opposite corral fence under his belly at the top of that last buck; Hank kept right on going for about three more feet, lost his hat in the process, and came down hard—so hard I heard him let out a long grunt from 25 feet away. He just laid there in the mud while the stud moved to the far side of the corral, stood there not moving, and watched Hank lying on the ground. I jumped down from the gate and ran over to where Hank was just starting to get to his feet. I helped him up, and he retrieved his hat. He looked at me and said, "The dirty s.o.b. tricked me. When he stopped at the gate, I figured he'd had enough, and I relaxed my hold on the rope. I sure wasn't ready for that last shot."

The stud was as nervous as a bachelor on Sadie Hawkins Day...

We walked over to the corral gate and stood there for a while. Then, Hank looked at me, grinned, and said, "I'm going to ride that stud if it takes all day." He got his lariat off the fence, and I thought, if it takes all day, that'll be okay, but more likely it'll take a whole week.

Hank threw the rope over the horse's head and slowly pulled it to the center of the corral. Hank stood there for a long time, looking and talking real low while the stud watched him. The only thing I heard of the conversation was Hank calling the horse a goofy-looking mountain goat with no brains. Hank then approached the horse, hand over hand on the rope until he could reach out and touch the stud. Hank patted him, slowly working along his neck, talking all the time. The horse was actually calm, and I said a quick prayer asking that Hank have more savvy than the stud. Hank kicked a toe into the stirrup and swung aboard real quick. Lo and behold, the stud never moved a muscle, and Hank just sat there, afraid, I'm sure, to urge him to buck.

After about three minutes, Hank relaxed his hold on the rope, and the stud took a few steps, stopping at the fence and looking back at the weight on his back. Hank seemed to know what was coming as he pulled back on the rope just as the stud started to buck again.

The stud bucked around the corral, but this time around, he stopped at the gate and just stood there, nervous as a bachelor on Sadie Hawkins Day, snorting some. Hank said, "Open the gate." I swung the gate wide open. The stud ran out the gate with Hank holding the rope real tight. The stud did not buck. He ran out into the hay field and then back to the corral where he stopped just inside the gate. Hank dismounted, lead the stud to the center post, and tied him up short. He removed his saddle and the rope from the stud's neck, patting him all the time. Hank told me later that someone had worked on the horse but didn't finish the job.

It took two more days of skittish slow riding, saddling, and putting the bridle on the stud before Hank felt satisfied. Four days after Hank started, he told Elmer to saddle up the horse for a few days, then to get on him for a day or two, and then to ride him.

He got a little more than he bargained for...

Hank rode off the next morning about sunup, heading south towards Roundup, Montana. I had watched Elmer give Hank ten silver dollars and an envelope as he left. I knew what was in the envelope but I never said a thing. The envelope contained a ten-dollar bill and a letter attesting to Hank's superior ability to ride and break broncs. Hank rode off, sitting tall in the saddle and humming a tune to his horse.

1946

Howie

When I first met Howie, I was sitting in the Greyhound bus depot in Billings, Montana, waiting for a bus home. It was 1946, and the war was over. People were moving around more rapidly than during the conflict. There were quite a few discharged veterans exiting and boarding the Greyhounds, heading for the homes they had left over the past five years. I had been sitting there on a soft pine seat for about two hours with nothing to do but watch people and read. Watching people is a thoroughly enjoyable pastime. Most people react differently when they are in transit, and their actions and attitudes change when they are in familiar surroundings. Howie was an exception.

Howie was just naturally gifted...

I was watching the front door when a small-statured fellow slid through the door and stopped just inside with his back against the wall. He was about five feet tall and extremely thin, clad in jeans, a clean, cheap cotton shirt, and army combat boots. He was clean-shaven and appeared to be about 50 years old. I gave him my undivided attention over the top of my paper. He stood by the wall for several minutes, surveying the occupants of the waiting room, and smoking on a short cigar stub. When he was satisfied, he glided towards the bench I was sitting on and sat down by the cigarette urn.

As I watched, he retrieved every extinguished butt from the urn and did it in such a way that nothing appeared to take place. His hand would rest on the arm of the bench for moment and then, like a flash of lightning, dart out and retrieve a handful of used cigarettes. He deposited them in his shirt pocket. When he was finished, he pulled out a medium length butt and lit it. Looking at me, he grinned and said, "Busy place." I nodded agreement. "My name's Howie," he said. I nodded again. I had to marvel at his cool. He seemed to be in complete control of everything he did.

He sat there smoking for about five minutes and then stood up and started towards the café adjacent to the waiting room. This I had to see. I followed. He was remarkable. Looking neither right nor left, he walked along the row of booths lining the wall. As I watched, he suddenly slid into one of them and disappeared from sight. I proceeded to the counter and sat where I could see him in the mirror. He was very proficient. He had picked a booth where someone had left a few pieces of toast and a partial container of coffee. As I watched, he pocketed the tip that was left and partook of the provided lunch. I watched as he left the booth and walked out into the street. He was good. His ability to obtain tobacco, lunch, and some change was undeniably the best there ever was. As I watched the waitress clear off the booth, I was sure that she did not know what had just transpired. I had to grin to myself.

Howie just got better with the passing years...

I met Howie again a couple of years later. Same place, same situation. However, this time he appeared more prosperous. Instead of sliding through the door, he walked in and sat down beside me. He looked at me and smiled, saying, "Busy place." A few of his front teeth were absent, and he lisped a little. I nodded at him. As I watched, he again cleaned out the cigarette urn, using a different method of operation. He had a lighted cigarette in his hand and, as he reached over to flick the ashes, he would palm a few of the longer butts. He didn't bother with the shorter ones this time.

Then I noticed the difference: standing by the door, back to the wall that Howie had used before and attired in jeans and a cotton shirt, stood a woman. She appeared unconcerned about the activity in the waiting room, but her eyes watched everything. When Howie left to enter the lunchroom, she followed a short way behind. Howie was a family man! I stood and watched them walk by the booths and slip into one of them. As I walked past their booth, I glanced down. They were partaking of a leftover lunch of potato chips, soup, and crackers.

1946

Friends

Ray and me was ranch hands on a spread up Big Elk way,
Branding steers and fixing fence and stacking wild hay;
Feeding sows and punching cows and working side by side,
Until that day of the rodeo when I fixed Ray up to ride.

Now I'd watched Ray at roundup time chasing ornery steers,
And I saw him ride an ornery bull after a couple of beers;
He seemed to ride like part of the hide of everything he rode,
Drunk or sober on horse or steer I'd never seen him throwed.

One Sunday morning after chores while Ray was healing slow,
I saw this ad in the Harlo news on the Wheatland Rodeo;
I read it through a time or two and knew that we could win
If I could figure out a way to get Ray entered in.

The paper listed out the prize for every main event,
There'd also be refreshments at the cowbells circus tent;
So sitting there in a tilt back chair I read the ad again,
While Ray just snored away the pain from drinkin' too much gin.

I studied hard 'til suppertime on how we'd win that dough,
Then I began to brag on Ray but I had to take it slow;
I talked to hands from other brands on how good Ray could ride,
And I figured out that we would win if I worked on his pride.

The week went by and we went to town the day before the show,
To meet some friends at the Stockman Bar and see the Rodeo;
I broke it slow that I had the dough for Old Ray's entry fee,
And Ray became the hero because he just couldn't disagree.

We got old Ray to the loading chutes a little after one,
And all his friends from the S Lazy T Ranch came to watch the fun;
But when I knew the horse he drew, I tried to stop the ride,
But Ray wasn't feeling any pain and he wouldn't run and hide.

They poured old Ray onto that bronc and screwed his hat on tight,
"Powder River, let her buck," he yelled with all his might;
They turned him loose on that cayuse and I had to turn my head
'Cause I knew that if I watched him, he'd plumb sure turn up dead.

Well, I finally looked and there he was riding like a pro,
He seemed to ride forever 'cause those seconds sure went slow;
He made that ride like part of the hide of that brown cyclone,
And when the ride was over, I was glad to be heading home.

I've seen old Ray a time or two since that day of the rodeo,
But he hasn't spoke or looked at me since he put on that show;
I guess I'm to blame, but just the same, I knew that we could win,
And maybe someday, he'll say, "Hi," and we'll be friends again.

1952

Just Good Friends

In 1947, while working for John Miller on the Top Hat Ranch above Two Dot, I was rebuilding and repairing a line fence that ran from the Big Elk River to the lower breaks of the Crazy Mountains. It was possible to drive a vehicle most of the way up the fence line, and I started at the top and worked down the mountain. It seemed that every winter the snow piled high on the fence, and the weight of the snow in the spring as it started to melt and slide downhill took parts of the fence with it. It bent quite a few of the steel fence posts over, leaving gaps where the cows could walk through and down along the foothills of the Crazies.

The buck was courting the cow, and had been for a year...

One Monday I loaded up some steel posts, a roll of barbwire, a post-pounder, a roll of plain iron splice wire, and some coffee, and started out along the fence from the Billy Donald Ranch. There were quite a few cows having breakfast along the fence, and they spooked as I approached in the old Ford truck. That is, all but one, who totally ignored me. She appeared to me to be trying to get through the fence and down on the Big Elk River. I stopped about 300 feet away and turned off the truck to have some coffee. I also wanted to see why she didn't cut and run like all the other cows. After about ten minutes, she started to walk along the fence toward a lone tree some distance away. I waited and watched a few more minutes, and I saw the reason the cow didn't run. Leaving the camouflage of a small group of trees, a large buck deer walked over to the fence and stood looking at the cow, nose to nose. I watched for about ten minutes, and all they did was stare at each other. The deer had seven points and was a husky-looking animal. It had a long scar on its neck.

Daylight in the mountains on the west side comes late and leaves the same way. I had a fence to fix, so I started the truck and drove towards the pair as slowly as I could. When I got about 50 feet away, the deer turned and ran towards the trees, but the cow didn't move until I sounded the horn. Then she slowly walked away. I spent a lot of time thinking about what I had seen, and when I returned to the ranch house, I told Alvin Berg what I had witnessed. Alvin laughed and told me that the buck was courting the cow and had been doing it for the past year.

I'd seen a lot of odd animal behavior, but that took the cake...

I told him I had never seen the likes of that before, though I had seen some odd animal behavior as I was growing up on the farm. We had a goose that followed my mother around whenever she went outside. We also had a big red rooster that slept in our collie's doghouse. And we had a neighbor whose saddle horse hung around with a small herd of sheep.

I knew the odd courtship was a waste of time for both parties, but I thought it was a good story for members of my family to listen to. I worked on the line fence splicing the wire for a whole week in June of 1948, and every day, I saw those two lovebirds standing at the same spot most of the day. One Sunday in July, I drove up along the fence to see if they were still friends. I saw the cow standing by the fence, and I parked about 100 feet away to watch the get-together.

I knew that the deer could easily jump the fence if it wanted to, but he never attempted that. The cow and the deer visited about 30 minutes, and then the deer turned and walked away. I returned a few more times to take a picture of the scene, but I never saw the deer again, though I did see the cow at the fence a few more times before I left to return to school in Roundup, Montana, the last week in August.

The cow waited for the buck, but he never came back...

In June of 1949, after graduation from high school, I drove up to the Top Hat Ranch with a friend to visit with Alvin Berg. He was the same quiet, sincere guy I worked with for two years. We visited for a while, and before I left, I asked Alvin about the odd couple's romance. He told me he had driven up along the fence quite a few times, but had not seen the deer since the summer of 1947. He said the cow showed up a few times, and when they brought the cows down for the winter, the cow was found down along the Big Elk River. They brought her down with the rest and never took her up to the grazing area.

L to R: Junior Bartlett, Al Anderson, Tom Anderson. April, 1949.

Alvin told me that, during hunting season in the fall of 1948, a large group of hunters had been in the area. He remarked that it sounded like a firing range in that area. He surmised that someone had harvested the deer for meat. My brother, Tom, later told me he had seen a seven-point buck in the back of a pickup parked at the Graves Hotel. It was during hunting season when he was up there in 1948.

I prefer to interpret that odd relationship as a chance meeting between two animals as close to each other as friends. I was privileged to witness something that very few people ever see. I still believe that buck was too smart to let a hunter get close enough to shoot.

1949

Little John Baird

I was working at Kibble & Case Cigar Store in Roundup, Montana, in 1945 doing everything but working hard—which meant working behind the soda fountain. This gave me the opportunity to do a whole mess of visiting with almost everyone who came into the store. Miners, cowboys, railroaders, and town folk—every day the variety of occupations and nationalities of Roundup patrons never ceased while I worked behind that counter. Roundup had begun to put on Fourth of July celebrations in 1945 after a short hiatus caused by the war. They had put on some events in 1944, but 1945 promised to have a dandy rodeo. The town grew overnight on July 1, and quite a few new faces looked out from under Stetson hats, and new and old scuffed boots were in the majority. The newcomers walked the sidewalks, patronized the eating establishments and local saloons, and really helped the local economy. Quite a few stopped in where I worked, and I became acquainted with some of the rodeoers clear through July 6.

He had run away from home when he was 11…
There was one new face that I'll never forget, and it belonged to a cowhand that was somewhat down on his luck and not too happy with the way the world was going around. He came into the

store the morning of the first day of July to buy some cigarettes. We only had a few cartons of Chelsea and Wings, and he chose to buy a sack of Bull Durham instead. I threw him a sack, and he readily opened it, rolled a cigarette, lit up, and took a big puff. It was evident that he had not had a cigarette for quite a while, and I watched him while he smoked that cigarette and rolled another. Then he sat down at the counter, looked at me, and said, "My name's Baird. John Baird."

I shook his hand and told him the name everyone called me, at least to my face, "Andy Anderson," and we shook hands again.

He looked at me for a minute and said, "I've also got a nickname around the rodeos—it's Little John. I don't like it much but it's better than Shorty." I asked him why the moniker, and he said, "Hell man, I'm five foot three inches tall, but with boots, I'm five foot seven. That ain't too short."

He sat there, smoking on the small end of the smoke, looking at me as if I was supposed to say something. The beat-up hat on the side of his head was really old, somewhat crumpled with a pretty good stain around the band, and almost wore out. He had the countenance of a man who had been outdoors for the most part. He also was tanned and wrinkled, and he needed a shave. He was wearing an old cotton shirt that used to be blue, frayed all the way around the collar. He sat there on the stool, and we visited for quite a while between customers. I learned that he was originally from Nebraska, down by the Fort Robinson area, and had been riding saddle since 1916 when he ran away from home at 11 years of age.

He had so many stories to tell...

He knew quite a bit about the Platte River area and had heard of the 1876 pioneers on their way West. He told me a few stories about some of the fights against the Indians on the Bozeman Trail that he had heard from an old pioneer named Mayor that he had met in Laramie in July of 1917. He said the old cowboy was 90 years old and still rode horses some, but he had seemed pretty frail aboard. He said that old cowhand had been all the way to the Fort

Hall area once and clear down into the Great Salt Lake country. He'd also been up into Virginia City, Montana, once and had made it back to Laramie, where he passed away.

John was in Roundup to ride in the rodeo and to try to win some money to get back to Wyoming in style. He was 41, had worked all the way to Canada, and would be heading back home in any case, after the rodeo—win, lose, or draw. He mentioned the Circle C Ranch up around Havre—I had seen Walt Colburn in Roundup once—and he told me about the Missouri Breaks country, where some Canadians ran some horses, and about the underground town in Havre. He had seen a lot of paintings in Havre hanging in the saloon with the *C.M. Russell* brand on them.

One dang thing after another...

He told me that the worst experience in his life happened in May the year before, when a friend had helped him round up a few head of horses in the breaks and try to trail them up into Canada. They did pretty good until they got to the border above Malta, Montana, when someone took a shot at him with a rifle, and the slug went through his left leg, through the stirrup strap, and killed his horse. His friend roped another horse and threw the saddle on him, and they kept going north. They only rode a few minutes, when a herd of Red Coats hailed them and put them under arrest for stealing commonwealth stock. After patching up his leg, they were both bedded down in the Crowbar Hotel, and the police confiscated everything they had including their saddles, bedrolls, and a pistol they had used to shoot rabbits with. Two days later, they were escorted to the border and severely warned never to cross the border again or they would probably get a free swing from the nearest tree.

They traveled south afoot until they caught a ride to Havre on a loaded hay wagon, where they found a job at the local stockyards, pitching manure and feeding hungry cows for a week or so. One night they "borrowed" a couple of used saddles, roped two scrub horses, and saddled up to head south towards Billings, intending to stop at Roundup and compete in the rodeo on July 4.

When they got to Roy, Montana, Carl, his buddy, headed west towards Lewistown, and Little John continued on south. He camped on a hill just about two miles north of town and hitched a ride into Roundup. He had left his horse staked out amongst some pine trees.

The first rock in the trail ain't too bad...

That was the darnedest tale I had ever heard, and I told him that he probably had to pay to ride in the rodeo. He looked at me and said, "I ain't got a solitary dime." He got up and walked out the door, stood by the curb, smoking on a hand-rolled smoke, and he sure looked alone. I could see his boots were run-down and scuffed up pretty bad. I thought then that John Baird sure needed a new ration of good luck.

After work, a friend gave me a ride up the highway where we searched for John's campsite. We spotted a small area that looked like a campsite. There was a fresh pork-n-beans can lying by some rocks that had housed a fire and some rabbit bones lying in the ashes. A shiny 30-30 casing was in the grass nearby, so we figured that John had fixed supper and left for parts unknown.

One of the last comments I still remember him saying was, "The first rock in the trail ain't too bad, but when everyone throws a few more in your way, it's tough to ride a straight trail." He never mentioned a family, and I never asked, and I figured the tale he told me was worth a lot more than a five-cent sack of Bull Durham.

1945

Louie's Howitzer

In 1952, my brother Tom and I were renting an apartment from a man named Jack Frazee in the Hedgemere Apartments on 7th Avenue North in Billings, Montana. We were attending Eastern Montana College, now MSU-Billings, in north Billings, and we shared our home with three other students—we all paid just $12 a month rent.

Our apartment was on the opposite end of the complex from the apartment of a man named Louie and his wife. He worked for the railroad and was a crotchety, rotund man who didn't liked anyone, even himself. He complained about almost everything. When we rented the apartment, we were given a set of rules to protect all the renters and they were more than fair. The no-no's included: no loud noise after 9:00 p.m.; renters' washing machines were sacred—if it wasn't yours, don't use it; no lady friends in the apartment after 9:00 p.m.; no men friends in any of the single ladies' apartments under any circumstances; and no snow on the sidewalk in front of your apartment.

We were totally innocent—that time…

These rules were fair and equal, and we strictly observed them, a lot better than most of the other tenants. There was a member of the fairer sex in one of the lower apartments who threw a knock-down-drag-out party one Saturday night, and the next day there were beer cans and debris on the front lawn. We were turned in a few days later as the culprits. We were totally innocent, but we got a warning from the landlord. When we received more than five complaints in one year, we were to be asked to move out. We never made the blacklist, but we did get four complaints the first year. Everyone who shared our apartment had jobs in the evening, and there was always traffic in and out almost 24 hours every weekday.

After suffering complaints and false accusations the first year, we had a general meeting of our "family" and decided to turn the tables on our nemesis, Louie, once and for all time. We discussed the fact that Louie could hear a mouse belch for 50 feet and hear a fly cleaning his wings for a block. Louie worked nights for the railroad and left for work every day in his Chevrolet car at 4:30 in the afternoon, with Saturdays and Sundays off. He always arrived home about midnight and parked his car right in front of his apartment, so we had to be extra careful, whatever we decided to do for retribution.

We weren't entirely innocent…

Now, I have to admit to a few itsy-bitsy infractions that caused some of the complaints. Once Tom and I had been soft-talked into streamlining a big yellow tomcat that was bothering our neighbor's little fluffy female cat that sat in their window all the time. The tomcat would sit on the corner of the fence behind Louie's apartment and carry on like a jilted suitor who had been getting some condolence out of a Jim Beam bottle. He'd meow and get into an occasional tooth and claw fight that could be heard for several blocks. After our corrective surgery, he wailed the blues for a day or two before he stopped.

We also had a racecar—a 1932 Ford Coupe—that we raced at the Wonderland Raceway. There was a big "100" painted on the side of the car, and it sounded like a locomotive needing grease when started.

Al Anderson and the 1932 Ford Coupe racecar. 1952.

Tom and I became the owners of a fighting rooster that could whip anything his size and probably every cat and dog on the block. His crowing made the birds exit their nests and made all the neighbors get a little upset. He was the ugliest critter I ever saw, with talons like hay hooks, beady green eyes, and a beak that resembled a yellow pitchfork tine. He was so ornery nobody thought he was a chicken.

The last apartment violation was the worst one. We parked our 1940 Chevrolet Coupe in Louie's spot, and he had to walk an extra 20 feet to his car. That caused a complaint, and someone told us that Louie bellered like a young bull fenced away from a whole herd of heifers. When his anger got up, he chewed the dickens out of his cigar, and I believe he swallowed it, piece by piece. His wife was quiet and pleasant, and I did not hear her say more than "Hello" in two years. Louie always parked his car so that he took up two parking spaces, but no one ever complained. One afternoon, he drove off with his lunch bucket sitting on the roof of his car, and it must have fell off on the way to work. When he came home, he woke up the owner and said we stole it. It so happened that some of the renters saw what had happened so we didn't get the blame for that. We told Jack that we weren't thieves—especially for two boloney sandwiches and a piece of pie.

We thought we should help Louie see the error of his ways...

One round table discussion laid out a series of "get even" plans. Letting the air out of one of Louie's tires was a priority. When he saw the flat tire, he was at a loss and had to call a service truck. We put blocks in front of his tires, but he saw them and kicked them away. We soaped up his windshield with some ivory soap, and he spent a good hour cleaning it off. He complained a couple times but there was no way he could pin it on us. This went on all winter of 1951, and when spring came, Louie complained that we had never kept our sidewalk clear of snow.

Most of the other tenants were fed up with him, too, and one dumped a bottle of henna in his washing machine so he wore colored undershirts for a month or two. His wife got angry because the henna colored the tub a mild orange, and it took quite a few loads of water to get it out.

Then one Saturday in 1952, Tom came up with the best stunt of all. Louie's car was like new, and Tom remarked that it was a shame that the car was in such good shape he didn't have to worry about it. Tom said that Louie's car exhaust was as tight as the skin on a grape and didn't leak at all and that cars had to expel the carbon monoxide from the gasoline to keep running. If the tail pipe became plugged, the car wouldn't run. It would probably start, then stop, and not restart. We all figured that a car that wouldn't start would give Louie something else to dwell on and leave our group alone. We all agreed that Louie was a nice guy once in a while, but didn't care much for college kids. Tom went into the kitchen and brought out a good-sized white potato and the broom.

Tom's idea was to put the potato into the tail pipe and push it up as far as we could, being careful not to leave any evidence of what we had done. We talked it over and decided we would do the good deed Sunday night or early Monday morning. When Sunday came around, we stayed close to the apartment watching Louie clean his car. He worked on the windshield for a long time, smoking a long cigar. When he finished, he climbed into the car and started it up, working the accelerator up and down a few times, and drove it around the block a few times. Then he parked it so no one could park in front of the car.

That was perfect because a big Chinese Elm tree was on the boulevard, hiding the back end of the automobile. It was around 1:30 in the morning when his lights were finally turned off, and we waited another hour to make sure he wouldn't catch us. When we felt the coast was clear, we retrieved our equipment and sat down on the street side at the rear of the car. Then Tom tried to insert the potato into the exhaust, but it was too big around. Tom took out his pocketknife and pared some of it off. I pushed the plug into the tail pipe, and Tom used the broom handle to push it up into the tail pipe as far as it would go, about 24 inches. We cleaned up the area and wiped off the back of the car just in case Louie had the car fingerprinted for evidence. After all the excitement of fixing the car, we couldn't sleep most of the night.

Retribution is sweet, oh so sweet...

We arrived home from college at 4:00 Monday afternoon and parked across the street so we could see what would happen. At exactly 4:15, Louie came out and climbed into his car, setting his lunch bucket on the seat. He tried to start the car, and it started for a second or two and then quit. Louie cranked on the starter a few times, but it wouldn't start. Louie climbed out of the car, stood looking at it for a few minutes, and then trudged off to work carrying his lunch pail. It was a long seven blocks or more, and he sure could use the exercise.

The next day, as we were heading out to school, Louie had the hood raised on his car, and a man with a tow truck was looking under it at the engine. I walked by and asked them if we could help, and they just looked at us. When we arrived back from school, the mechanic had the tow truck hooked to Louie's car, getting ready to tow it away. I walked over to see what was going on, and I heard the mechanic say, "When I get going, shove the car into third gear and let out the clutch." Louie looked like a racecar driver, hunched over the steering wheel, gripping the top of it with both hands and chewing on a cigar.

We stood and watched as the tow truck towed the car away, and we heard the rear wheels as Louie let the clutch out. They had moved only about 50 feet when we heard what sounded like a cannon go off. The tail pipe expelled the potato, and it whistled past us like an 88 mm Howitzer shell, traveling a good half a block before it came down to the street. It was doing about 50 miles an hour. If anyone had been in the way, the missile would have knocked them out of their drawers. When the noise began, the tow truck operator hit his brakes, and Louie didn't. He plowed into the tow truck at about 25 miles an hour and came to a grinding halt. The impact pushed in the grill and bent the bumper and both front fenders, breaking out the headlamps. Louie must have made contact with the steering wheel, as his cigar was smashed flat against his mouth. He was just sitting in his car, both hands on the steering wheel, staring straight ahead with the stub of the cigar in his mouth. We heard the tow truck operator say, "How come you ran into my truck?"

The operator had a bigger truck come and tow the car to the garage, and Louie went into his apartment. We never saw him for several days. Tom retrieved the big missile from the next block, and we hung it on our wall. I guess Louie finally figured out that, as the world goes around, so goes everything—including retribution.

We next heard from him one Saturday in December when Louie came to the apartment and handed Tom a good-sized paper plate loaded with cookies. He said, "My wife figured you bachelors might enjoy a few cookies. They're homemade." We thanked him, and when he left, we enjoyed a few. We also noticed that the chocolate one had O-R-E-O stamped on both sides. But we ate the whole bunch, and they were tasty. We never received another complaint.

1952

Cowboy's Prayer

While doing chores at the end of the day
I've stopped to bow my head and pray,
To just thank God for being here
Able to live without knowing fear.

To think of eternity and what it means
In terms of life and unfilled dreams,
And the better things I know I'd do
If I could start over and begin anew.

For man's life is short in terms of years
An unmarked pathway filled with tears,
While the joy of love and newborn life
Outweighs the pain of toil and strife.

And when I've prayed, I make this vow
To live God's word as I know how,
For I know that when my journey's run
I'll be judged for things I've done.

1952

Matrimony — Almost

In the fall of 1948, I returned to Roundup High School as a senior and was hired by Fergus Graham to work at Staunton Chevrolet on Main Street in Roundup. I was the only person working at the service station from 5:00 p.m. until I closed it down at 10:00 p.m. During those five hours, I performed some ongoing chores and sold a lot of gasoline to travelers heading both north and south on Highway 87. In between customers, I studied some, visited some with local patrons, and met one whale of a bunch of new friends.

In the first part of the month of November, I met a ranch hand from the Miles City area named Raymond. He stopped in to buy gasoline one night on his way from Forsyth to Great Falls, Montana, to visit a friend. We talked for about one hour, and he mentioned that he had worked up around Two Dot and Harlowton in 1945. Actually, he had worked at two different spreads that year, for Dana Martin and for the Fox Ranch east of Harlowton.

Raymond had stars in his eyes and a song in his heart...

Raymond told me that he was heading up to Great Falls to see his lady friend, who had moved up there the past summer. He hoped to talk her into being his "side kick," as he put it, and marry up with him. He seemed to have pretty high aspirations for an unemployed cowhand. He had worked down around Miles City, Montana, all summer and had saved all of his pay. He was driving a 1941 Ford that was well-kept, and his Stetson and boots looked new. He was about six feet tall, ruggedly handsome with an infectious grin, and talked like a true cowboy.

He showed me a picture of the young lady, whose name was Doris, and she was one of the prettiest ladies I had ever seen. I asked Ray where he had met that pretty little dark-haired lady with lots of freckles. He told me he had been to a dance at Cushman, Montana, one Saturday night, and when he saw her sitting on the sideline, he went all to pieces. He had watched her for one dance, and then he asked her to dance. He said he wanted to grab her and kiss every one of those freckles, envelope her is his arms like a cloak, and spirit her away.

I looked at him standing there grinning and asked him if he ever told her that. He just shook his head no, paid for the gasoline, climbed into his car, and left. In the middle of the next week, I was getting ready to close up the station when Ray drove into the station. He came into the office and visited for a few minutes about the trip from

Forsyth. He mentioned that his friend Doris was coming to Roundup on Saturday to see her aunt and that he would be able to be with her over the weekend. He came into the station the following two days, and on Friday, he reminded me that he would meet the Greyhound Bus the next day down by Dinsmore and Graves Drug Store to gather up the prettiest little filly in Montana.

Pretty big plans for a pretty small budget…

Ray planned to meet the bus, escort her to his car, and deliver her right to the front door of her aunt's home on one of the streets west of Main Street. I told him I would be working Saturday night, and maybe he could bring her, the love of his life, by the station so I could meet her. He agreed and left, heading for the Palace Hotel where he was holed up waiting for Saturday. The next day about six o'clock in the afternoon, he drove into the lot and ushered his girlfriend into my office. He introduced us, and I had never before seen a lady who looked like Venus De Milo with all of her clothes on.

When she smiled, it almost did a job on my heart, and I thought that Ray could have whipped a whole herd of other suitors just to see her smile. They left after a few minutes; I figured that Ray was probably the luckiest cowboy on two feet, and I hoped things would work out for him.

Two days later, he stopped by and mentioned that he was going to drive Doris up to Great Falls, Montana, but right then he was heading for the barbershop for a trim before he met her parents. When he came back, he smelled like a whole grove of lilac bushes and was some upset. He said that the stupid barber was an apple short of a full basket and had over-done the lilac water after the hair cut. He seemed as nervous as a male pooch at the vet's shop and tried to wash some of the smell out in the drinking fountain. I figured that the lovebirds had better get hitched in the near future before Raymond developed a nervous disorder.

The size of the bankroll won out in the end…

The last time Ray stopped by to see me, he was on his way back to Miles City alone. We visited while I filled up his car with gas, and he told me he'd been working harder than a lone ant trying to feed a colony. He had been trying to convince Doris to either elope with him right then and get married by a Justice of the Peace at the courthouse, or just come back to Miles City with him so they could be together. He said that, after he got through begging, pleading, and crying some, he found out that she had another friend she was hoping to tie the knot with. He was the son of a rancher living up along the Marias River and had money. He had a brand new Ford pickup, and he had a whole herd of red cows that they were going to sell. He said the guy's name was Fred and that he bought Doris gifts she adored and Ray just couldn't afford. I never saw a man so upset and so down in the mouth in my life.

Before he left, he said he'd miss Doris something fierce, but from now on, he'd keep clear of pretty girls. He said that Doris was a genuine cowgirl and a real woman inside a shirt and Levis, but could also cut you up pretty bad with her tongue and smile while doing it. He climbed into his black Ford, cranked it up, and pulled out into the street—right into a truck hauling logs to a sawmill. The truck hit the car and caved in the passenger side, pushing it about 20 feet. Ray climbed out of the car, looked at the mess of metal, threw up his hands, and walked away. I never saw Ray again after that fiasco. The city hauled the car to the dump, and it sat there for several weeks. One day a wrecker from Forsyth came and towed it away.

Maybe Ray did get the best end of the bargain...

The next time I saw Doris, it was at the Days of '49 Rodeo the next July, and she was with a big, hefty cowboy. She walked right by me on the street with a small dog on her arm and never even looked my way. I figured that Ray was a lot luckier that he thought when she left him the way she did—at least she didn't get the chance to mess him up.

The man she was with had a superior air about him as he towered a couple of feet over her head, and he was dressed pretty good from the heel of his boots to the Stetson hat tipped back on his head. I couldn't help but think that the toll of upkeep on Doris would weigh pretty heavy later on and might become a big burden.

After the rodeo was over that Saturday night, a large dance was held in the Legion Hall on First Street West. A few of us went to the dance to see what was going on. Between dances, the participants just walked around the dance floor until the music started again. I was standing by the bandstand when some of the men started to walk out the door, and pretty soon, most of the men were outside. I walked out to see what was happening, and there in the middle of the street, nose-to-nose and not saying a word, stood Doris' husband with his hat pushed back on his head looking down at a huge coal miner. He appeared ready to punctuate some of the cuss words that flowed between the two.

Apparently, the miner had asked Doris to dance, and her husband objected. Not knowing the custom of dancing with ladies if they concurred, he had pushed the miner away and wouldn't let Doris dance with anyone else. I heard one of the men say that Doris had egged her husband on some and appeared to be totally enjoying the coming event. I knew the miner from my time at Kibble & Case, and I would have bet a year's pay that he would win the argument. He was tougher than a 15-year-old bull that had lived on a diet of sagebrush, locoweed, and bunch grass. The cowboy couldn't back down—Heaven forbid! The brand of "coward" would be a horrible epithet on his back for the rest of his life, but then again, that life might be much shorter anyhow, unless the miner took pity on Doris' husband.

I had been around cowboys, miners, and railroaders all my life, and I knew the cowboy didn't have a chance. I was right. After the doctor finished the job of patching him up, he took Doris away, and I never saw either of them again. But I figured that, had Ray been at the dance, he would have enjoyed the outcome to the fullest.

1950

Melville Saturday Night

There are probably a lot of people who have never heard of or been to, a little town south of Harlowton called Melville. Boy have you missed a unique experience and a later opportunity to brag about going to a dance in the Melville bar. Actually, Melville is not a town in the acceptable definition of town in that all I ever saw in Melville was a storage shed and a pretty good-sized bar. Two Dot is larger than Melville, but I don't think that really matters. What matters is that Melville is situated about halfway between Harlowton and Big Timber on Highway 191, about a half hour's drive. It sits right in the middle of cowboy country, including the Beehive Property.

We also threw in a 20-year-old guitar in case the music failed...

One Saturday in July of 1947, Alvin Berg asked three of us cowhands working on the Top Hat if we wanted to go to a dance. Asking unmarried, 20-year-old, hard-working cowboys a question like that was like asking us if we wanted breakfast. Our motto was to do anything that was relaxing and fun, after a week of ten-hour days putting up hay on the ranch. We all gladly accepted, and after supper, the three of us climbed into Alvin's black Ford car, dressed to the nines—that is, clean Levis and an almost clean shirt, boots cleaned off good on the back of the pant leg, and a Stetson hat that was creased, crushed, and sweat-stained to show we were working cowhands. We also threw in an old guitar so we could have music if the electricity failed.

The ride to Melville took awhile, and we drank the two six-packs of Budweiser beer we had bought at the Two Dot Bar. Bill Trautman asked Alvin where we were off to, and when Alvin said Melville, Bill hollered, "Good luck, men. Stay sober if you have any guts, and hurry back."

We got to Melville about 8:00 that night, and you could see the lights of the bar and hear the music about a mile away. The parking area around the bar was packed with cars, old and new, parked every-which-way around the bar, as if the patrons couldn't wait to get into the swing of things. There were license plates from Bozeman, Lewistown, Big Timber, Harlowton, and Roundup pasted on the automobiles. Big Timber was the most prevalent of them all. The doors and windows of the bar were wide open, and it sounded more like a free-for-all than a dance. Alvin stopped us at the door and told us to be careful and to stay sober. That was like asking a chicken not to scratch for bugs.

We got into the bar and joined the crowd dancing and having one heck of a good time. One of our group, Ray, started drinking Cabin Still booze and pretty soon asked John to go bring in the guitar so we could have some "good" dance music. He figured to give everyone a real treat. John went out and brought in the beat-up old guitar and sat down on a long bench along a wall. He started to bang out chords, and they actually sounded pretty good. He was not feeling too much pain and hollered out, "*Old Shep*, everybody." That was a disaster when everyone started to sing. It sounded like a roomful of irritated, upset Herefords. John tried another called *Don't Fence Me In*, and that sounded a little better.

The bartender kept sending loaded drinks over to the bench to try to shut the singers up. After all, the jukebox was quiet, indicating no revenue for the bar. It wasn't too long until the singers couldn't carry a tune in a gunnysack, and the music started to sound like a coyote caught in a trap. But they stuck at it until one of the bigger cowhands grabbed the guitar and put it over behind the bar. John pushed him when he came back, and the cowhand grabbed John by the collar and belt and literally threw him off the bar porch. Everything was quiet for a while, and then John came staggering back into the bar, sat down on the bench, and promptly fell asleep. His snoring sounded like a growling animal. A couple of the guys propped him up against the wall. The rest of the cowhands tried to sing *You are my Sunshine*, but the melody was gosh awful, and the words weren't in sequence. The bartender sent over a few more drinks, and at the same time, one of the cowhands brought the guitar back and gave it to one of the singers. He tried to play the darned thing, but the bartender had cut all of the strings off and disabled it. It wasn't too long until most of the singers were beyond any coherent singing. A few minutes later, the jukebox started up again and dancing began. We had a great time that night and met a bunch of new friends. John and I had tried to count the attendees, and we figured there were about 50 couples and about 20 singles in the bar.

There were no other arguments, and as the evening wore on, everyone seemed to have become friends. The highway patrol could have cited about half of the partygoers that night. I later heard that the owner was happier than a clam at the revenue from the dance. He closed the bar at about 3:00 a.m. and started to leave for Big Timber, but some dirty dog had cut all of the valve stems on his car, and he had to catch a ride home. That was the only time I was in the Melville bar.

Hangovers the next day had to be rampant—the bar ran out of beer at closing time. The bartender's wife wasn't feeling any pain, as she was happy as a meadowlark in the morning. And there were 12 inebriated cowboys, courtesy of the singers.

This was the first dance I had ever attended where there were no fistfights over anything—just noise, dancing, and drunks. I have only one positive statement about dances like that. While some cowboys and cowgirls make handsome couples, most of the cowboys are not even pretty, while most of the ladies are prettier than a blue sunbonnet. Cowboys are pretty lucky when a lady consents to help him run his string out to a successful conclusion, wading beside him through problems and circumstances stickier than wet Powder River gumbo.

1948

Bachelor Quarters

In 1951, I enrolled in Eastern Montana College in Billings, Montana. Pursuant to this, a group of five of us students attending Eastern got together, and we rented a basement apartment about six blocks from the college. The rent for the apartment was $60 a month, and each one of us paid $12 a month, which was the best rent in the area for students. The apartment was furnished with two double beds, one day bed, and one stacked set of bunk beds. The ceilings of the rooms were only eight feet high, and the water registers for heating the whole area were mounted on the ceiling. There was very little space, only about 30 inches, above the top of the bunk to the registers, and the water lines ran all over the ceiling from the furnace on their way to heat the upstairs of the Hedgemere Apartments. One register was right over the top bunk of the stacked beds, and a good-sized person would have been hard put to move around very much.

It was like a train depot...

All five of our aspiring group moved into the apartment and helped each other with their belongings. Closet space was divided up,

Al Anderson.
Eastern Montana
College. 1951.

and space was assigned with total agreement of all concerned. About a week later, another student asked to move in with us. We made room for him in the closet, and he was given the top bunk—right under the water register. He wasn't overly happy with that assignment, but there was no other place to put him.

We all settled in comfortably, and the apartment was like a train depot—someone was coming or going 24 hours a day. The apartment was never fully occupied between 5 a.m. and midnight. Early risers had early classes, so from 5:00 a.m. on, sleep was impossible. We set limits on radio use and times of operation. We had routines for showers, studying, and cooking. Some took meals at Eastern, some had early morning jobs, and some participated in sports. We respected each other's rights and set only one rule—no ladies after 9:00 p.m., and it was enforced by all.

Everything ran smooth until one Sunday in November of 1951. Winter had followed a cold fall that year, and the steam heat was turned on the last week of October. The apartment was warm, and everyone was content with the way we lived. The sleeping arrangement was okay, with Fred the only critic, since he had the top bunk.

He said he could hear the water rushing through the pipes on its way upstairs. He said he had to go to the bathroom more than usual, and he knew that it was the sound of running water that triggered the urge. Since Fred drank a lot of inexpensive beer like Great Falls Pale, Highlander, and Butte Beer, I figured that was the real cause and told him so. He did cut down to about six cans a day and felt better.

Groaning like a horse with colic...

In late October, Fred had set his alarm clock for 5:00 a.m. one Monday morning to go up to the college early for something. He parked the clock on a small table next to the bottom bunk, and when it went off, he leaned over to turn it off and fell headfirst down onto the table. The table broke all to pieces, and Fred ended up with a cut on his head and a black eye. That morning everyone was up at 5:00. After using some choice, profane adjectives to describe our apartment, he calmed down and became docile once more. He fixed a small shelf on the wall next to the top bunk to put his clock on, and things went fine for about two weeks with no disasters. His eye turned from black to purple and finally healed up.

One Saturday around 3:00 a.m., one of the occupants shook me awake and said that Fred was groaning and carrying on pretty bad. We went to check, and I also heard Fred moaning. There were three others asleep in that area, so we couldn't turn on the lights to see what the problem was. We had a flashlight, so we got that and turned it on Fred. He was lying on the bunk on his back, sweating profusely and looked feverish. His face was whiter than a clean sheet.

While we were looking at him, he groaned and put his hand on his right side. Looking at me, he said, "I think I'm having an attack of appendicitis. I've got to get to the hospital."

We shone the light on Fred's stomach, and sure as hell, there was a large, round inflated area about the size of a saucer on his right side. He groaned again like a horse with the colic. He put his hand on his stomach, and looking at me, he said, "God, Al, I think I'm having appendicitis attack. I've got to get to the hospital."

That darn bed tried its best to kill Fred...

I called the Deaconess Hospital and told them we had a medical emergency that would need a surgeon because Fred appeared to have a ruptured appendix. We were only three blocks from the hospital, so I told the nurse we'd be there in about five minutes. We pulled a light jacket on him and took him up to the emergency room in my car. He kept muttering something about a broken appendix and peritonitis. We took him in the emergency room, and there was an orderly waiting with a stretcher table. We helped put him on the table, and the orderly wheeled him into an examination room.

They were in there for a long, long time—about an hour and a half—before the doctor came out to talk with us. He looked at me over the top of his glasses and frowned. I thought, "Holy Crap. They've taken him into surgery already."

The doctor sat down next to us and told us the complete procedure he had put Fred through. He said, "Well, I've got to tell you that that young man was pretty scared. He moaned a lot on the way and finally quit when helped onto the exam table. He was sweating and holding his right abdomen. We put a gown on him and x-rayed the area. The first x-ray showed nothing at all, so we ran it again. That one indicated a pretty good-sized mass on his right abdomen, about five inches around. I asked him when he first started to feel the pain, and he said in the middle of the night. I had another doctor look at him, and after perusing the x-ray and visiting with Fred, we all concurred that it was a major scald from hot water dripping from the steam heat air valve above his bed."

During the course of the night, the valve had dripped water on his abdomen every few minutes, and had scalded the area, but it would be fine in a few days. Talk about relief! Fred came walking out of the examination room grinning from ear to ear. His jacket was open, and he had a dressing on his wound. He said he felt like a new man. Needless to say, we had the landlord get the leaky valve fixed.

Fred moved out and into an apartment with a friend. Fred came down a few days later and said to me, "Al, I told you guys I didn't like that top bunk. That darn bed tried its best to kill me."

1951

The Planting of Billy Joe

We are gathered here, the preacher said, to pay our last respects
To Billy Joe who met his fate while hanging from his neck.
It just ain't right to leave a man, his solemn voice droned on,
Without a fitting place to rest, once his Spirit's gone.

The Good Book says that it's a sin to steal what ain't yourn,
And if Billy Joe had read the book, he just forgot the words.
Judge ye not lest ye be judged applied to man alone,
So let us bow our heads and pray for Billy's journey home.

Poor Billy Joe was a wild lad, who grew up free of rein,
A troubled soul in this wild land of misery and pain.
Now we all know, God rest his soul, that Billy loved to live,
And his unkind deeds of robbin' folks is what we must forgive.

Barleycorn was the ladder down, he climbed it rung by rung,
Courtin' Satan on the way until he was finally hung.
Ashes to ashes and dust to dust but man's soul travels on,
And some of us a standing here will meet him when we're gone.

I recall that day his mother came into our little church,
Holdin' on to Billy's hand so tight it must have hurt.
She came a lot from that day on, with Billy at her side,
And in their eyes was sorrow that they just couldn't hide.

Little Billy lost his daddy when he was only four,
A cattleman had shot him dead in the Rincon County war.
Now we plant the troubled lad in this shallow lonely grave,
And the cattlemen who hung him will follow him some day.

1952